i was a spirited child, said the man

with the donkey head and the rabbit ears.

you could go this way, or this way,

or this way, he said. or some other way.

this gunpowder could be used for fireworks

and this electricity could be used for art.

and art could be everywhere, he said.

art could be everywhere...

W I

W A R R E N

E.C. GRAHAM AND KEVIN HANEK

FOREWORD BY HILARY JAY | INTRODUCTION BY PHILIP YENAWINE

N K

MULLER

BAHDEEBAHDU

PHILADELPHIA

Paul Schneider's essay, *An
Artist and a Designer Who Found Their Niche*,
reprinted with the permission of *The New York Times*; Feral
Willcox's poem, *i was a spirited child*, reprinted with permission of
the author. All images ©2008 by Warren Muller unless otherwise noted:
Images appearing on pages 3, 53, and 59 © John Carlano; images appearing on
pages xi–xiv, xx, 12–14, 54–59, 86–89, 106–109, 116, and 119 © Brad Fowler; images
appearing on pages vii–ix, xvi–xix, 6–7, 26, 104–105, and 128 © Robert Hakalski;
image appearing on page 66 © David Matthews; image appearing on page 33 © Esteban
Michel; images appearing on pages 52–53, and 113 © RJ Thornburg; images appearing on
pages 8 and 42 © Isaiah Zagar. Published by bahdeebahdu, with the generous assistance
of Lis and Michael Kalogris, and additional assistance from Leslie and David Matthews.
A portion of the proceeds from this publication will go to the KatherineAlexandra
Charitable Foundation, which supports and promotes the arts, healing, education, and

ISBN 978-1-60585-508-0

BOOK PRODUCED BY
KEVIN HANEK AND E.C. GRAHAM

Manufactured in the
United States of America

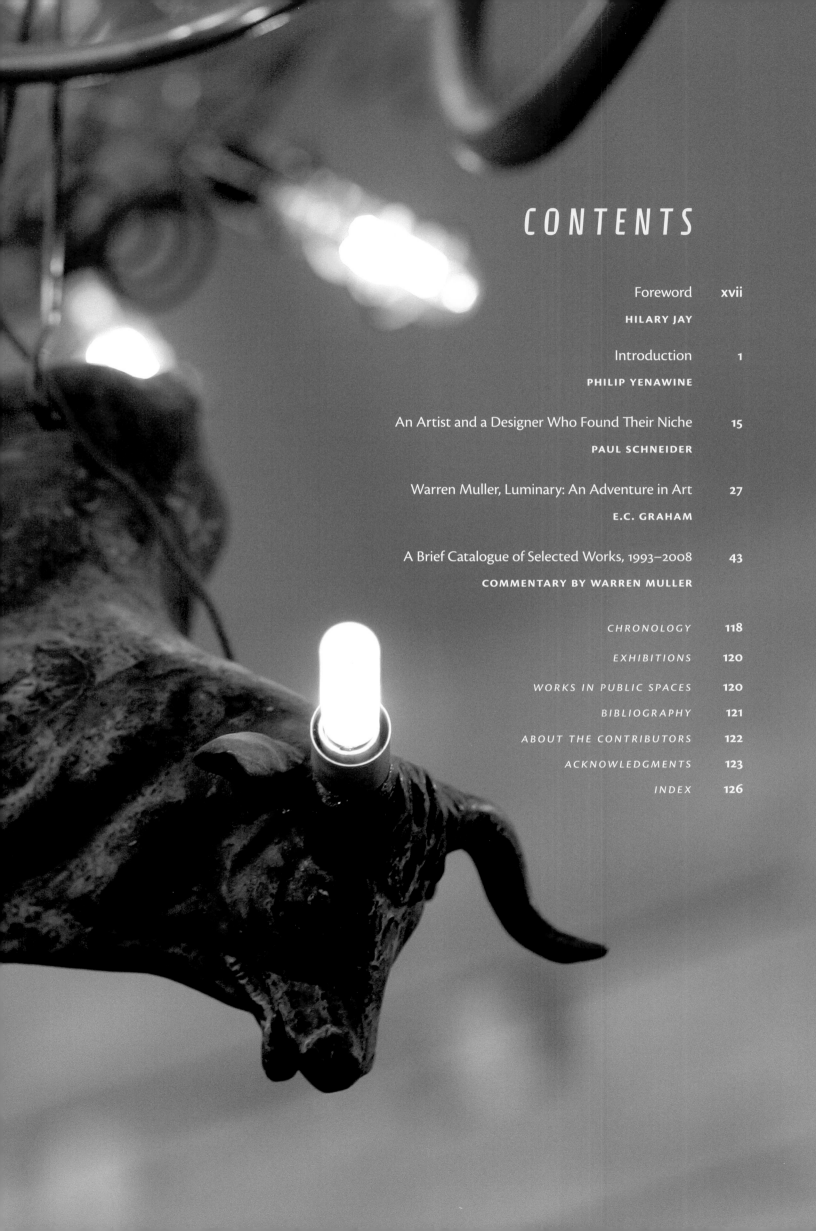

CONTENTS

Foreword   **xvii**

HILARY JAY

Introduction   **1**

PHILIP YENAWINE

An Artist and a Designer Who Found Their Niche   **15**

PAUL SCHNEIDER

Warren Muller, Luminary: An Adventure in Art   **27**

E.C. GRAHAM

A Brief Catalogue of Selected Works, 1993–2008   **43**

COMMENTARY BY WARREN MULLER

CHRONOLOGY   **118**

EXHIBITIONS   **120**

WORKS IN PUBLIC SPACES   **120**

BIBLIOGRAPHY   **121**

ABOUT THE CONTRIBUTORS   **122**

ACKNOWLEDGMENTS   **123**

INDEX   **126**

and circles of rabbits spinning in kitchens

shining down pleasant opinions on breakfast.

and bright blue chickens scratching in illumination,

art could be everywhere... and tractors swinging

gracefully above golden bottles of scotch with skies

where they harvest the random words of drunkards

and sow them deep in the future where they awaken

in the songs and sonnets of woodland birds...

FOREWORD

HILARY JAY

EXECUTIVE DIRECTOR, THE DESIGN CENTER AT PHILADELPHIA UNIVERSITY

T HE DONKEY-HEADED MAN with the incandescent arms in the gallery window stopped me in my tracks. I laughed out loud. It was the early 1990s, and I was a city editor then for Metropolitan Home magazine, on my beat in Philadelphia's Olde City, looking for stories and designers with the potential to transcend the local and speak to the zeitgeist of the times. The door was open, the invitation clear. This was Warren Muller's world, his studio, his showroom, his performance space.

Unbeknownst to us both, I had walked in on the early stages of what would be an artist's twenty-year exploration with light and objects. Muller's work was almost mild-mannered, whimsical (always, and to the core), but somewhat restrained compared to today. In these ensuing years, Muller has let loose with his baton, sometimes casting out big, broad symphonic strokes, like the lyrical chandeliers in the Philadelphia Building, other times creating floating explosions of light, like his "Minimasterpiece," with a 1964 Austin Mini at its center, suspended 20 feet overhead.

It's taken years for Muller's story to come out, and a number of writers to tell it. It's all here in these pages: growing up in the Bronx, the son of a drycleaner; decades of artistic training and experimentation, the "aha" moment in Chinatown. In here lies an examination of the way Muller's work echoes trends in modern art—avoidance of convention, for one. There's the tale of finding the perfect Pocono Mountains farmhouse and the metamorphosis taking place there; and stories of friendships and collaborations that have influenced Muller's creative journey.

There's no categorizing what Muller makes. Chandelier comes to mind. But in fact, this work is not about function. If these pieces happen to bring light to darkness, that's very nearly a happy accident. Then, as now, the work signifies an ever-escalating worldwide trend: objects that defy a neat definition as art or craft or design. They simply refuse to be put in a box and labeled. Muller's work transcends these categories, reaching beyond aesthetic appreciation, to become culturally reflective and intellectually inspiring. He keeps good company today—contemporary artists and designers such as lighting designer Ingo Maurer, the Dutch collective droog, Marcel Wanders, Philippe Starck, all who create works that conjure a dream and a wink.

Curiously, this man with the slightest of grins is hiding a six-foot-tall laugh. He looks at the multitude of cast-off vinegar bottles, trashed buggy wheels, tossed rebar rods, rusted carpenter's tools, and sees something else in that detritus—a grown-up's sandbox, an invitation to play. Through his magical manipulations of objects and light, Muller translates notions of romance, mystery, exoticism, even mirth. He conjures sculptural assemblages by performing a sort of mischievous alchemy that turns randomness into order, order into art.

WM: "My workshop in the new gallery space on North American Street in Philadelphia. We awakened the morning of February 13, 2008, to the news that there had been a serious electrical fire in our gallery on Cherry Street. Nearly everything in the gallery suffered damage from smoke and water. Ironically, we were in the midst of preparing for a move to this space just a few weeks later."

INTRODUCTION

PHILIP YENAWINE

FORMER DIRECTOR OF EDUCATION, MUSEUM OF MODERN ART, NEW YORK

A GLANCE IS ALL IT TAKES. We grin and think, "…Never saw anything like that before…" We recognize the categories, of course—light fixtures or chandeliers—but such designations are too lame to describe what Warren Muller makes. In the way that architect Frank Gehry has reshaped our expectations of buildings, Muller has exploded notions of the look and function of lighting. Not simply illumination, certainly not mere aspects of décor, his zany, commanding constructions either make or take over the space they inhabit/dominate. Suddenly, lamps are fun. And space is transformed.

Unique as Muller's concoctions are, his avoidance of convention is one hallmark of the modern era generally. The drive to innovate has propelled all arenas of activity, and it was clearly a driving force in art and design throughout the twentieth century. The modernist poet Ezra Pound, quoting no less a thinker than Confucius, challenged his 1920s peers with the admonition: Make it new! While tossing a gambit, he was also mirroring what he saw already happening.

Merely a few years after the turn of the century, Pablo Picasso and Georges Braque found ways to confound our eyes and minds with new stylistic strategies on canvas and paper. Their experiments, eventually labeled Cubism, spearheaded further thinking about what was possible in art, and little of it had to do with tradition. Wassily Kandinsky in Europe and Arthur Dove in the United States are both credited with the total abandonment of reference to the real world in their paintings, creating abstractions of colors, lines, and amorphous shapes.

In an even more extreme gesture, Marcel Duchamp jettisoned art materials altogether, placing ready-made objects, little transformed, in galleries, saying art is more about ideas than things; conventional craftsmanship simply holds one back. If I say a urinal is art, he claimed, then it is. His iconoclasm had a profound impact on his contemporaries and most who followed. In direct response, his anti-art stance ushered in the movement called Dada, whose proponents championed nonsense over logic, order, and convention. Accidents came to play an important role in Surrealism, art that found inspiration in the subconscious and dreams more than in the world we share. Surrealists such as Joan Miró and Jean Arp tried to eliminate conscious decision-making while creating. Remember: only half a century earlier, the Impressionists were derided as heretics for thwarting studious realism. By the time some Surrealists determined their compositions by chance and mined their unconscious for imagery, the art world, at least, had embraced radicalism.

WM: "The couple who commissioned this piece told me they wanted a reason to spend time in this room. The final piece did not include the ladder or myself…"

In other words, by the time Warren Muller found his way into a studio, the phenomenon of creative inventiveness had a long lineage. As he came of age, there was even a trend among artists working in clay—normally associated with traditional forms and functions—to abandon its use as a medium for making useful objects. Experimenting with technique, these artists were not inspired by traditional means of forming pots but by what was happening in other media, such as painting. Peter Voulkos, for example, translated the active, aggressive gestures of expressionist painters into rough, energetic ceramic sculpture. Moving in another direction, Robert Arneson's self-portraits—funny, nasty, sexualized self-parodies—were a clay artist's appro-

priation of Pop Art, itself an antidote to the austerity of much modern art, architecture and furniture.

Muller was similarly inspired by Pop Art and intrigued by experimenting with clay, but his take was more like that of painter James Rosenquist. He was sufficiently intrigued by everyday images and objects that he incorporated them into his work with eclectic abandon. The practice of including actual objects from the real world in art originated in the studios of Picasso and Braque as they were developing Cubism. Along with drawing, they began to paste bits of newspaper and other ephemera onto their images, an idea Picasso further developed in sculpture, casting such things as toy vehicles or handlebars in bronze to make pieces that

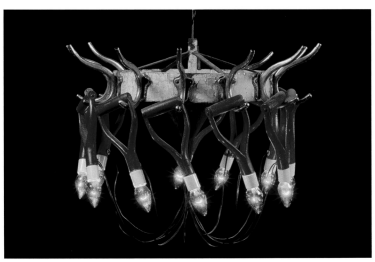

OPPOSITE, CLOCKWISE FROM UPPER LEFT Pablo Picasso, *Bull's Head*, 1942, bicycle seat and handlebars, Musée Picasso, Paris, Réunion des Musées Nationaux/Art Resource, NY; Peter Voulkos, *Rocking Pot*, 1956, stoneware, Smithsonian American Art Museum, Washington, DC/Art Resource, NY; Claes Oldenburg, *Screwarch Bridge (State II)*, 1980, etching and aquatint, The Museum of Modern Art, New York, digital image © The Museum of Modern Art/ Licensed by SCALA/Art Resource, NY.

ABOVE Jean Tinguely, *Hell, a Small Start*, 1984, varied materials including salvaged metal, ferns, and an electric motor, Musée National d'Art Moderne, Centre Georges Pompidou, Paris, CNAC/MNAM/Dist. Réunion des Musées Nationaux/Art Resource, NY.

AT LEFT Marcel Duchamp, *Hat Rack* (top), 1917/1964, replica created under the direction of Marcel Duchamp by the Schwarz Gallery in Milan, Musée National d'Art Moderne, Centre Georges Pompidou, Paris, CNAC/MNAM/Dist. Réunion des Musées Nationaux/Art Resource, NY. Warren Muller, *Marcel du Lamp* (bottom), 2000. The first in a series of works in tribute to Marcel Duchamp.

ABOVE James Rosenquist, *Spring Cheer*, 1942, lithograph, private collection, ESM-Ed Meneely/Art Resource, NY.
OPPOSITE Warren Muller, *Animal Dreamland*, 2003.

WM: "This was a rare opportunity for me to work in collaboration with Isaiah Zagar and RJ Thornburg for a designer showhouse installation to raise funds for the Pennsylvania SPCA."

otherwise resembled things and creatures we would encounter in real life—bulls, or goats. Slyly humorous and innovative as these works were, they only hinted at the extent to which Duchamp and others would take the idea.

By midcentury, Robert Rauschenberg was collecting junk from the streets and combining paint, detritus, and incongruous objects into assemblages whose meanings can only be guessed. His fellow enthusiast for the stuff of our lives, Claes Oldenburg, made versions of things we use out of impossible materials: canvas electric fans or vinyl telephones. In one hugely influential instance, he created a store of useless useful things, and Warren Muller took note.

The use of old farm equipment, wheels, gears, and other machine parts took Muller in the direction being explored by Jean Tinguely, that of monuments and public works sculptures made from castoff industrial materials. Tinguely's influence brought Muller full circle in his conceptualization of the light sculpture.

Muller's own generative impulses are as idiosyncratic as his Pop Art forebears, and his particular voice more clearly contributes elements of intentional whimsy and humor. His delight in transforming things we use without thinking—his search for the magic in, say, the hammer lying on his workbench, as he recently said to me—has been an irresistible impulse. He reexamines the ordinary, puts things where they don't belong, and gives new life to banality and a new charge to us as viewers. Whether creating in clay, performing, or assembling his lighting devices, he is determined to take nothing for granted, and therefore gives us the chance to experience the extraordinary.

Celebration
of Shopping
for that special
object that
symbolizes
a journey
Isaiah / Julia
Vickey
R. J. & War.
in
Mexico

a birth day gift
3/18/2004

DISTANCE FROM EVERYTHING from you

LIPS

holding flower

WARREN'S NEW FELT HAT

and if you had a basket, or a bucket,

or an upside down metallic thing, you could

gather glass flowers and they would light up like fireflies

on spheres, on planets suspended in the glow of wonder.

is it animal, mineral, vegetable, kitchen chair,

or do you even care when you're lost in a trance

of milk bottles shining likes specks of phosphorous

floating in the ocean...

AN ARTIST AND A DESIGNER
WHO FOUND THEIR NICHE

PAUL SCHNEIDER

REPRINTED FROM *THE NEW YORK TIMES*, JUNE 23, 2006

T HE MASSIVE BLACK WALNUT TREE rising majestically behind the house was a very good sign, for it meant that one of Warren Muller's three requirements for a country place had been met. And it was even before Mr. Muller, an artist, and his partner, RJ Thornburg, an interior designer, had walked through the front door of the 19th-century farmhouse they were checking out in the Pocono Mountains, in Brodheadsville, Pennsylvania.

"I told RJ that there were only three things I really needed to be happy," Mr. Muller, 60, explained recently. "A fireplace, a bath and a good tree to hang my hammock."

Mr. Thornburg, 50, who once created rooms by the thousands for Disney and other corporate clients, and who today is one of Philadelphia's most sought-after residential interior designers, could easily add a fireplace and a luxurious bathtub to the house if they ended up buying it. But a tree like the walnut, with its large branches strong enough to hold both ends of a hammock, could not be manufactured. It had to be found.

Found objects play a large role in Mr. Muller's life, though the tree was somewhat unusual in that he had an idea of what he was looking for before he found it. His art, which is not simple to describe, is mostly electrified installations that range from playful chandelierlike fixtures built of teapots and samovars to large conglomerations of rusty farm implements, bright orange broom brushes and glass busts of dead presidents.

Most of his pieces are commissioned for specific spaces, but many of those that are not are for sale in Mr. Muller and Mr. Thornburg's gallery, bahdeebahdu, at 309 Cherry Street in Philadelphia.

Mr. Muller's works are constructed almost entirely from everyday objects that he collects on regular pilgrimages to flea markets, junk stores, Home Depots and the like. And though he often knows generally what he needs—"I'm looking for something that could make an elegant pair of sconces," he said, holding up as possibilities two wood-and-steel mole traps that looked disturbingly like some kind of medieval chastity device—more often than not, his collecting is done without a finished product in mind.

Occasionally material even shows up unbidden, like the collection of vintage pedal cars that arrived in a crate sent by friends on vacation in Asia, with a note saying, "We thought you might like these." Mr. Muller thinks they might be useful in a piece he's creating for a Mini-Cooper dealership.

WM: "In the country, we take a lot of walks. There's space to breathe, and plenty of room for imagining our dreams and goals. It's a place to regenerate and let go."

In a way, the house on the wooded lane in the rolling, bucolic hills of Brodheadsville fits into the unbidden-treasures category. About three years ago, Mr. Muller and Mr. Thornburg began a typically relaxed search for a place outside the city. Their first thought was Bucks County, Pennsylvania, where they had visited and had friends.

But after a few excursions with real estate agents, they realized that the prices in Bucks County and other similarly popular Philadelphia retreats were more than they were looking to spend, at least for the kind of place they were hoping to find. "All we could afford were these little houses with no land, really, and no outbuildings," Mr. Muller said.

So when a friend came into the gallery talking about her place in the Poconos, a part of the world neither Mr. Muller nor Mr. Thornburg had ever seen, they were intrigued enough to say, "Well, if you hear of something that sounds like us, let us know."

The word came the next day. She had in fact seen a place that seemed to fit the bill—a three-bedroom, about 1,800-square-foot house on a hilly three acres in Brodheadsville, about 25 miles north of Allentown, and roughly the same distance from the New Jersey border. Best of all, perhaps, the sellers were motivated to make a quick sale. Mr. Muller and Mr. Thornburg decided to make a stop

there on their way up to a summer rental in Provincetown on Cape Cod.

"We were trying not to seem too excited as we walked around," Mr. Muller recalled. "We didn't want the sellers to know how much we liked it. But we pretty much knew it was great the moment we got out of the car. And then they said, 'Oh, and do you want to see the barn and garage across the road?' and we said, 'You mean those are part of the property, too?' We didn't even know until then."

By the time Mr. Muller and Mr. Thornburg got to Provincetown, they had decided to make an offer, and by the time they got back from their vacation, they had a deal (they wouldn't disclose the price). "We were saying to ourselves, 'Oh my God, what are we doing, are we out of our minds?' "

To see the house today is to know that they were in full possession of their senses, as well as the energy and taste to transform a place with a lot of potential but not much else into a home with a clean, modern style and a generous supply of creature comfort.

The kitchen, with its limestone floor and lava-stone counters, and which is hung with art made by friends, is now entirely elegant without having lost any of the coziness of a traditional farmhouse kitchen. Mr. Muller's required bathtub was added, of course—a deep, free-

standing affair with a second-floor view out to their garden-in-the-making. A new fireplace for the living room completed the primary wish list.

After that, removing the old ceilings to expose the beams and wide floorboards above, the addition of a second-floor deck, and the conversion of what had once been a mudroom into a sunroom, were just gravy.

In certain choice locations throughout the house, Mr. Muller's own work appears. Over the table in the dining room, for instance, hang three chandeliers of iron, wood, and glass. The central one consists primarily of a sharp and gracefully curving set of industrial calipers that look hungry themselves.

Over the mantel in the living room the effect is softer: a row of fifteen hooks, each with a teardrop bulb suspended from it. It reads like an inverted candelabra, or a friendly jack-o'-lantern grin.

Like most authentic farmhouses, this one was built in stages. The result is not unlike Mr. Muller's own creations, in which old, new, borrowed and incandescent pieces are fused into elegant new wholes that seem both to tell stories and to refuse to give up their secrets.

"I love the history that hides in everyday objects," Mr. Muller said. "A history that you know is there but that you can never really learn." It's as if to him objects—houses, rusty pitchforks, bent bugles and the like—have personalities and lives of their own that bring them periodically into personal interaction with people who are patient and open to what Mr. Muller calls the "interesting things that come our way when we aren't really looking for them."

Even the hand-carved columns by the house's entryway arrived in the usual unusual fashion. "I was standing here on the porch one day not long after we bought the house, and a friend called out of the blue all the way from India and said, 'I'm in this amazing market that's full of columns—do you need any columns?' And I looked at the post I was standing next to and said, 'Well, now that you mention it, let me get my tape measure.' "

Two years in, the work is by no means done. In addition to the house, the property has a barn that will eventually become Mr. Muller's studio; a large garage with an attached workroom that will become Mr. Thornburg's studio; a smokehouse that may become a sauna; a springhouse that still houses the pump for the spring water down by a spring that looks for all the world like Monet's garden; a chicken coop that may again become a chicken coop; and a two-seater outhouse whose future is still undetermined.

But there seems to be no hurry: the outhouse will surely let them know in good time what it intends to be.

ladle oh ladle oh ladle

oh colander in sieve in gigantic tea basket—

tell me oh tell me oh tell me a tale

of liquids in kitchens dripping and pouring and spilling

gather yourselves up in the air and shine

on the wrenches and ratchets, hammers and hatchets

the ropes and rasps and handles and fans

slurped up by tornado and spun until golden, until becoming

constellation in a black sky of imagination...

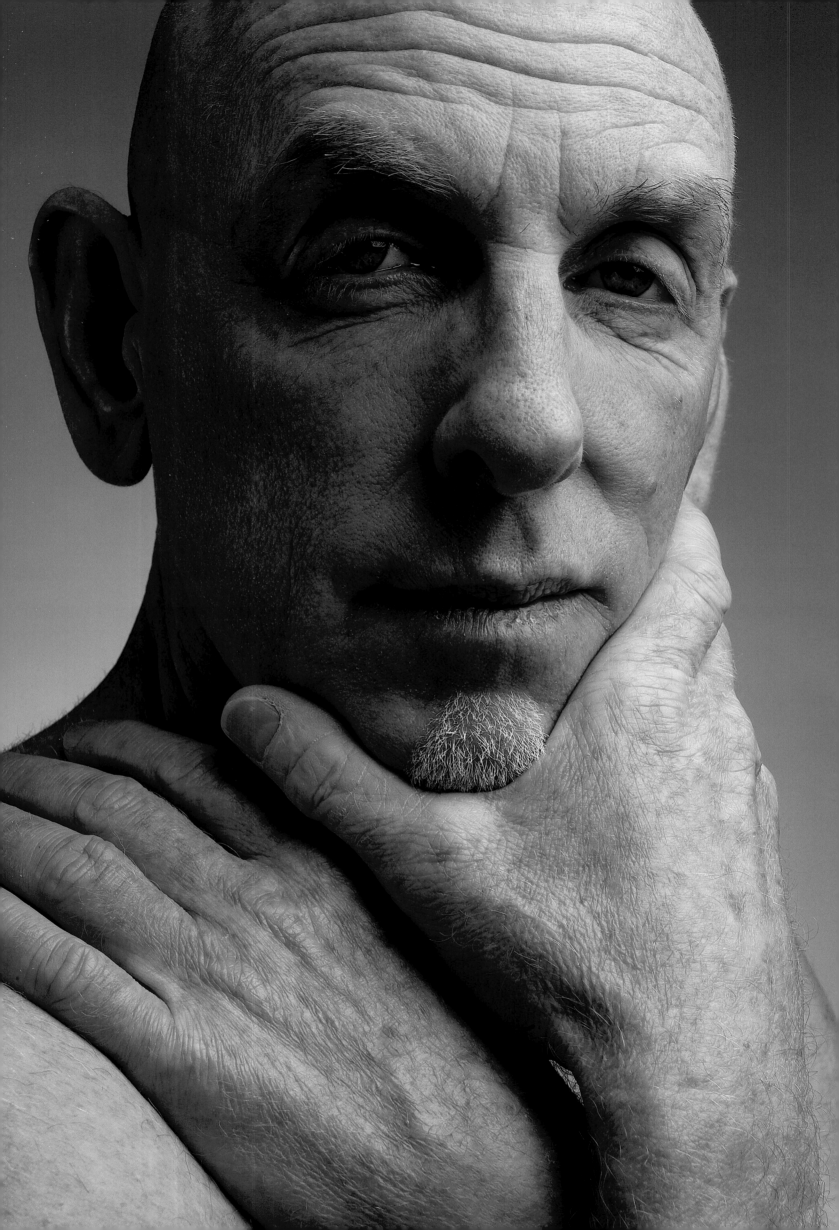

WARREN MULLER, LUMINARY: AN ADVENTURE IN ART

E.C. GRAHAM

When you start on a long journey, trees are trees, water is water, and mountains are mountains. After you have gone some distance, trees are no longer trees, water no longer water, mountains no longer mountains. But after you have traveled a great distance, trees are once again trees, water is once again water, mountains are once again mountains.

— ZEN TEACHING

T HE JOURNEY OF an artist is a journey of perspective. By this long road, perspective undergoes a transformation, seeing things first as they appear, then as they are underneath their form, then more fully to include both, so that although the trees seem to change shape on the journey, what has truly been transformed is how the artist sees them. This journey began for Warren Muller in the 1950s Bronx. Images spring to life from Muller's childhood in this predominately Jewish enclave of newly arrived Eastern European immigrants: the five-story walk-up, the gossip and scoldings in Yiddish, the sounds of salesmen canvassing the neighborhood, singing out their offerings—"wah...duh...me-lon" ... "I cash... I cash clothes..."—and street-corner violinists playing melancholy, old-world tunes. The sound of the Bungalow Bar ice cream buggy would send children running to the apartment windows, their mothers hurriedly counting change to put in buckets which they would lower on ropes for the five-flight journey down. A sharp tug on the rope from the driver signaled that the ice cream was ready to be pulled up. But cheerful interactions and colorful sounds didn't mask the fact that money was tight and work hours were long; a child growing up in that neighborhood learned to enjoy life with very little. On lazy afternoons, young Warren would stare down from the family's one-room apartment, taking in the city street below, endlessly fascinated with the performance of spontaneous interactions of neighborhood life.

Growing older meant more time spent at the family's dry cleaning business, sorting through piles of clothes and making deliveries to neighbors, who always had a plate of cookies and a story to share. In summers, the hot presses made the shop feel as oppressive as a boiler room, but the workers, who mostly came from the South, masked the hardships of their labor through singing and storytelling. The adolescent Muller 's exposure to their oral folk tradition would have a profound and lasting effect on his own storytelling. He saw how those stories could act like a comforting balm, and a beacon to light the way in the darkness of a toilsome existence.

WM: *"A portrait of me taken by my friend, the photographer Robert Hakalski, in 2005."*

The enterprise of cleaning clothes is, in a sense, an act of redemption: the sullied, the secretive–all are deposited there, and afterward, the cleaned, the renewed, the covered-up secrets returned, with a crisp storefront smile. And for a boy privy to these secrets, the impression that perception makes all the difference between something being viewed as worthless or valuable revealed clearly to him that everything possessed its own carefully concealed story, and that value is only a matter of perception.

One wonders, given Muller's creative response to this environment, if the British film director Michael Apted, best known for his "Up" series of documentary films–– based on the premise, "show me a seven-year-old, and I'll show you the adult he will become"—might have been able to recognize the potential artist in this watchful boy who sorted clothes and listened to the workers sing away their burdens. A boy who, when no one was looking, would burrow into the unclaimed clothes rack at the back corner of the store, emerging as a tattered, silk-pajamaed prince, or a Russian spy, invisible to his enemies in a long, oil-stained trenchcoat, or an adventuring scientist in a white smock, in search of the last of a species of rare insect, or some other character suggested by what he found there.

This theater of unclaimed clothes, the old Yiddish men who told outrageous stories to one another between card games, and the color and texture of his childhood streets all served as elements of inspiration, eventually finding their way into the performances which Muller now began to give from a small New York storefront.

His first audiences were left puzzled by the curious hodgepodge of characters summoned from his past. These still-green attempts at performance led Muller to realize that in art, as in any journey, when the road becomes blocked, you might need to take a side path, while keeping your gaze on the main route. On a walk in Chinatown one day, Muller noticed a display of hundreds of Chinese porcelain teapots, stacked in impossibly high rows and identically aligned so as to show off the indigo chrysanthemums painted on their sides. At bargain prices, he bought several boxes of the teapots, and immersed himself in their study, experimenting with various combinations of them in sculptural arrangements. Experiments like this, along with Muller's early work with lighting and

prop-making, which began as an adjunct activity to his performance pieces, now began to take center stage.

Muller's formative years coincided with an era of neglected cities in the East, abandoned by a fleeing middle class whose appetite for suburbia matched their aspirations for upward mobility. It was a unique time for artists in America, who, for a song, could either occupy or purchase outright entire buildings in her most famed cities. Nowhere was this more the case than 1970s Philadelphia, whose nineteenth-century prosperity now gathered dust, and who had been all but left for dead when she began to be reclaimed by, among others, artists. And her ambitious early life as an industrial town had left behind some monumental relics; a new generation of artists began to discover and take advantage of the bonanza of huge, empty buildings in which they could live communally and make art.

Self-portrait, nine years old
WM: "I made the background from various seed packets.
My Aunt Helen was the keeper of my pompadour."

Art Prints Reg. U. S

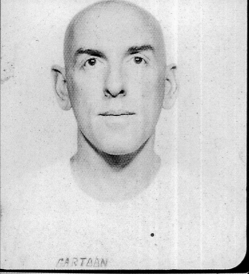

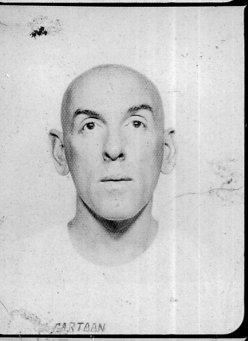

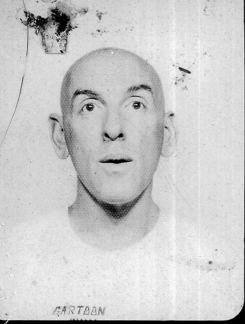

Besides the growing opportunities for these pioneering artists, Philadelphia's abandoned industrial core offered a treasure trove of raw materials, various odds and ends that once fueled the city's production. The deserted factories, naval yards, textile mills, ice plants, and the like, blackened with century-old soot, were like giant cathedrals to Muller and his friends, who discovered there the industrial-sized winches, calipers, hickeys, and hooks that once built the most impressive inventions of the age. The dramatic history of these tools was evident to anyone who would remain still long enough to observe them in their glorious rot. But to a young artist with a peculiar sensitivity to objects, the early-American buildings were forgotten museums exhibiting a visual cacophony of remnants, each of which was endowed with a unique story patiently awaiting an opportunity to be told.

The pulleys and switches, the staples and copper tubing, the metal straps that connected things yet to be conceived or created were stacked meticulously against the floor-to-ceiling shelves of the abandoned men's clothing store where Muller had claimed his space. Sharing the same space, Group Motion, a dance company co-founded by Manfred Fischbeck, Brigitta Herrmann, and other East Berlin choreographers, occupied the lower floors of the building for their studio and living experiment. Muller began filming the group in rehearsals and performances, and in a short time he was both lighting the stage and dancing with them, exploring a type of movement which became a foundational part of his work.

Group Motion's dancers created kinetic sculptures that embraced audience members into their choreography, transforming the usually passive viewer into an active participant in the dance. Fischbeck, who would later become a mentor for Muller, choreographed evolving geometrical patterns whose completion extended outward into the audience, so that if viewed from above, the dancers and audience members could be seen as connected by invisible lines in a larger constellation. Muller evolved with the life of Group Motion, going from documentarian and set lighting designer to dancer and back again. His participation as a dancer gave him an understanding of principles of movement that focused on the concept of spontaneity as a key to a door, unlocking the fertile contrast between still and explosive expressions of energy. Muller took note of the various movements of the dancers' bodies: the arcs, the sharp lines, the limits and the abstractions and sublimations that sculpted these pliable bodies in motion.

The activities used to train these dancers became the first patterns for Muller as he began building his light sculptures. Though these early works were not motor-driven kinesthetic creations with whirling parts, they did contain undeniable movement in their shape and assembly, highlighting a single form by using supporting bodies in a backdrop of movement around it. This technique of juxtaposing these contrasting elements suggesting varying degrees of motion resulted in newly generated forms, allowing the observer to complete the creation with an imaginary dotted line.

Self-portrait in photo booth, 1962
WM: "I had bright red hair back then. My mother bought me a green plaid coat which went great with my hair."

These asymmetrical forms are more interesting because, unlike whole shapes, they promise our imagination further movement, revealing themselves to us from within the form itself, guiding our eye in the direction the creator wishes us to go, and pushing observers to become more active participants. During Group Motion performances, new bodies would find their connections to ones previous to them, building on a constellation of interconnected, yet independently willed movers. Called a crystallization technique, the dancers formed a core whose collective impulse echoed out from the stage to the far corners of the space, sending a shock wave through the audience on the ripple of their movement.

Muller mastered this technique in his light sculptures, taking it a step further by applying these concepts to the motion of light. The moving human body served as a starting point for thinking about movement in light. He began to observe certain contrasts.

He thought about his lover's face lighting up with pleasure, and how that soul was the light of his life. He thought about bringing the truth to light, before the end, before lights out.

– JOHN MUSALL

Light possesses boundless possibilities; it can be either diffuse or concentrated, weak or intensified, soft and filling in its movement, or harsh and brittle, shattering like tiny shards of glass. Light can shoot through certain objects while being repulsed sharply by others. With the speed of a clap of thunder, light can burst onto a stage, flooding it to reveal naked forms, or rise slowly out of darkness, obscuring edges and cloaking substance. As light changes in intensity and creeps over surfaces along the curves of a body, it chases back shadow. Varying in its color, intensity, and angles, it can be expressed as dance.

The soul's distinct connection with immortality is best disclosed by danger, or quick calamity. Like lightening on a landscape, exhibits sheets of place not yet suspected, but for Flash and Click, and Suddeness.

— EMILY DICKINSON

Using the industrial-sized metal coat racks that had been left behind in the men's clothing store, he experimented with these concepts, creating loosely braided light fixtures, which hung like grapes from a wire vine, emitting light from multiple and variously colored bulbs. But the sculptures seemed to beg for more freedom to move. The search for how to play with light necessitated the discovery of a means by which to support it, that is, utilizing the aesthetic of the light source itself as inspiration and motivation.

Around the period of his collaboration with the ceramic artist, Michael Biello, Muller began to employ hollow containers in his fixtures, like the teapots, which now poured streams of light from their spouts. The coat racks would support early and crude mobiles, built along the same lines as the teapot sculpture, housing the light and becoming a curious beacon of sorts, a prototype for experiments to come.

Both of Muller's parents, upon reaching their sixty-fifth birthdays, died within one year of each other. He had watched them work fifty-one weeks a year, hardly pausing to enjoy their lives, and they had done so for over forty years, hoping that their sacrifice would pay off the day they retired. That day never came for them, and Muller concluded that if he didn't make his "someday" today, it might never come at all. He redoubled his commitment to pursue his art, as if his life depended on it, by "stalking the muse." This curious insight reveals something about the source of our inspiration: the muse likes to be courted, danced around, teased out, and given a chance to lead. Having learned from dance, Muller decided to "dance around the muse, to attract her, then take a step back and let her lead." In a tango with the opportunities that came his way, Muller teamed up with Biello and bought a building, founding a studio in which the sale of ceramic "light objects" would cover their expenses, while Muller continued further artistic experimentation with movement, light, and sound.

Early in his creative journey, Muller realized that in art, originality counts. Film, dance, theater—each, easily the commitment of a lifetime, could have led him down a path yielding less brilliant results. Instead of pursuing any of these art forms as ends in themselves, Muller combined these interests into a unique and original pursuit: the light sculpture, which would be defined by his evolving understanding of performance, movement, and theater. At this stage of his development, Muller chose to pursue a unique artistic path rather than work in a more conventional established art form, distancing himself from the scrutiny and constraints of the established art world.

A great cultural bias exists in contemporary society, whereby the seriousness and dedication of individuals who pursue multiple interests is called into question, or worse, they are judged to be dilettantes. This verdict has cost many a young artist the sense of freedom to innovate and explore new directions. Muller recognized that confining himself prematurely to a specific creative discipline would impose limits on his artistic growth. Specialization, the younger sibling of generalization, is thought by some to be the surer route to achievement, but while following that path may bring some rewards, it's also an undeniable detriment to the development of those artists who thrive on contrast and variety as the impetus for creation. Yet these rival interests and seemingly divergent practices, if faithfully pursued over the course of a lifetime, can merge into a coherent whole. Individual strands are finally seen as constituent threads in a larger artistic fabric, and the true significance of their pursuit at last becomes apparent.

The chance meeting of the artist Isaiah Zagar, who became a significant influence and one of Muller's greatest sources of inspiration, was one such strand. Zagar fiercely pursued a journey of spontaneity as expressed in art. Asking permission from no one and working outside of established art circles, he created a new modern folk medium with both architectural and political relevance with his mosaic sculptures and tile reliefs. Zagar would go on to become one of Philadelphia's most renowned artists. The iconography of his mosaics, echoing that of the Catalan artist Antoni Gaudí, burst onto the scene, or rather over it, like a colorful new skin covering entire buildings. Zagar transformed Muller's view of chaos in art and the value of fearlessly venturing into the realm that exists between craft and art, folk and political, and redefining the perception of worth and the aesthetic value of objects, finding broken and worn everyday elements, and making them extraordinary.

Zagar's interest in any experience for the sake of art led Muller to embrace the new possibilities that the presence of chaos in creation offered— chaos isn't something unintelligible or unmanageable, merely unpredictable. Chaos in art functions much like chaos theory in physics or mathematics, in which scientists assert that the flapping of a single butterfly's wings could affect the outcome of a hurricane, as each of the tiniest links on a chain of chaotic events affects the direction of the adjoining links, cumulatively shaping the outcome. Likewise, each step of the creative process is recognized for the impact it exerts on the evolution of the

finished piece, with the awareness that the subtlest change could drastically alter the final creation. The final product is revealed as the sum of many tiny cumulative steps. A variable dynamic, chaos creates tension, expresses movement, or in the excited state of turbulence, breaks up motion, so that a less predictable order emerges.

Chaos was, for Zagar, as close to performance art as one could get in the muralistic art world. His teams of workers collected the unlikeliest of materials to be assembled with his guiding aesthetic, making wall apparel, ceiling apparel, and monuments. Overlaying many concurrent working lines of information and communication, Zagar was not concerned if his works overwhelmed or

overstimulated the viewer. In fact, he operated from an underlying belief that, like a child spinning himself around until he reaches a state of dizziness, visual overstimulation can effectively alter the mind and free the imagination. These creations, outsized and composed of random elements, made the building façades a mesmerizing and alluringly grotesque portraiture to contemplate. Zagar's performance-art orientation as regards working with still objects now began to exert an influence on the direction of Muller's light sculptures.

Chandeliers evolved as a means of expanding the amount of available light in the cavernous interiors of cathedrals, at a time in history when most individuals didn't

have the means to light after dusk. Although the forms of chandeliers throughout history have varied considerably across the progression from candle to incandescent bulb, a chandelier is defined in part by the effect its position in the room imposes upon the light it emits. The geometric patterns of the highly refractive, multifaceted glass pieces which began to be hung from chandeliers have been largely symmetrical in design, made from ever more brilliant materials, but whose effect on light was to slice and scatter it, resulting in new asymmetrical patterns of illumination piercing its symmetrical reflection.

The electric light bulb revolutionized the chandelier, giving it increased potency but, some might say, arrest-ing its aesthetical development by forcing all other design considerations to capitulate to this new centerpiece. The overenthusiastic response to centuries of dimness was a torrent of glaring artificial light, which transformed the formerly naturally lit spaces into little more than sun-less boxes under an unrelenting electric gaze. Industrial designers would take the concept to its nadir with white popcorn ceilings and the unremitting (and distinctly un-natural) glow of long, fluorescent tubes overhead, reflect-ing nothing save a metallic dullness and the raw power of the bulb. This feverish attempt to eradicate shadow resulted in spaces in which a cold, surgical glow was the order of the night, and increasingly, the day as well.

Muller's designs exploded conventional notions of light sources by multiplying and contrasting them in his works: alternately softening and sharpening the light, creating myriad points within the same sculpture where light could dialogue with itself, and which the objects that housed the light did as well. In his efforts to dissect and manipulate light in his sculptural works, Muller took existing concepts of illumination and did away with the conventional limitations imposed by the bulb.

Muller's artistic journey was defined in part by his unforgettable teachers. His early years taught him a sense of the absurd and the sometimes tragic humor to be found in everyday life. His time working with Manfred Fischbeck was a lesson in playing with light and endowing objects with movement, as well as connecting them to their environment. His collaboration with Michael Biello taught Muller the creative opportunities, as well as the practical realities of making objects to house light. RJ Thornburg, Muller's interior designer-partner, taught him how to conceptualize ever-broader settings in which his chandeliers could interact with other objects, recontextualizing his art within new interior settings. And Isaiah Zagar taught Muller the limitless possibilities in embracing found materials for unbounded, outrageously conceived art. Zagar also encouraged Muller to challenge the art world establishment and expand the possibilities of what could be accomplished when the concept of creating art is predicated upon living life at the nucleus of a wildly exhilarating, subatomic view of spontaneity. Extraordinary art could be made from castoff objects, the crudest and most forgotten materials could be wrought into sculptures, and the techniques for producing great art could be achieved with Everyman's toolbox.

The sculptures speak to people in places where they don't expect to encounter an artistic experience, a workingman's art for Everyman. Only after this delicious first sip has been swallowed does the viewer begin to absorb the deeper and more subversive implications, namely, if mundane everyday objects and rubbish can be magically transformed anywhere into "art", what does this say about those things on which society does place a high value?

— DEBORAH SCOBLIONKOV

Echoing Duchamp's declaration that all objects could potentially be contextualized as art because art is how one perceives, Muller came full circle, not only redeeming objects and techniques considered artless and craft-oriented, but in reorienting these items and outfitting them with light, he redeemed our perception of them once again as objects of value and desire.

Exploring the balance, the angles, the volume and geometry of each object, Muller began to twist, turn, and invert these objects in space, filling them with light, then perforating them so as to spill that light, growing brass arms and legs to connect them, mapping ever greater constellations of the absurd and beautiful. Pulling light sculptures strongly in the direction of conceptual art, he began to juxtapose familiar objects in unfamiliar syntheses, the ugly with the beautiful, a beaming light sculpture populated with objects that individually were judged to be worthless.

When he finds them at garage sales, in industrial equipment supply houses or used junk stores, the worth of most of these ordinary-use objects has already diminished or disappeared entirely—they are sometimes offered as little more than scrap. Before they find their way into Muller's sculptures, their paucity of value has been measured by what the item fails to provide in terms of beauty, or comfort, or efficiency. Once deemed no longer useful and dead to their original purpose, these objects will find themselves on a shelf for resale, or more often in a trash bin, a landfill, or an incinerator. Some are broken into pieces or repurposed for parts, but many are left intact and simply forgotten. If most people in the world can claim ownership of hundreds or even thousands of articles, then the number of objects that undergo this life-cycle of usefulness must be astounding, exponential as it is to the world's entire population.

It requires a patient receptiveness which extends far beyond the world of other people into that of cast-off drill bits and ceramic figurines. Muller was simply waiting for something to call out to him. Waiting for a hundred-year-old industrial caliper, for instance, to confess to anyone who was willing to listen that all its long life of labor measuring tolerances in the machine shop, and all those decades afterwards of retirement in some back shed, it was always saying to itself, "if 1 could only do this all over again, 1'd be an artist."

— PAUL SCHNEIDER

From another standpoint, a sculpture created from reclaimed objects can be viewed as a metaphor, an awkward reminder of how we perceive the concepts of usefulness and worth as applies to our fellow humans, in whose death the measurement of the worth and value of their past life is now evaluated in hindsight. As with people, so too the imperfections in our objects—their existential quirks—take on a certain novelty for us once they have been released from their original purpose, able at last to be viewed with a new degree of objectivity. The memory of their defects fades in the light of this transformation and newfound relevance. When viewed and engaged by a particular kind of artist, one with a well-considered sense of intrinsic worth, the recognition of this relevance in an object is transformed into art.

Although a discussion of the life of an object may seem absurd, it is in fact the basis upon which we conscript things to the world of art. Whether created from primary materials or ingeniously assembled from piles of dimly forgotten objects, life, in artistic terms, comes from the imaginative breath, from the artist whose unique perspective endows the lifeless entity with new meaning and character. Muller's manner of assembling and illuminating a sculpture conspires to endow a bucket of castoff objects with a conceptual existence—and a practical life to go with it. Flirting with us, ignoring us, or playing irresistibly with our curiosity, these unwieldy sculptures have the effect of transforming light into performance.

Bamonte describes one piece as "curved copper tubing [which] meander[s] off and eventually end[s] up in a frenetic polycentric dance of [the] rusty, painted, falling apart, held together by ropes or wooden clamps, of glass objects, often having floral-like forms in many different colors that create a kind of enchanted garden without roots or gravity."

Spectators delight at Muller's use of ordinary objects whose inescapably symmetrical designs are suddenly jostled into asymmetrical arrangements, giving each piece a provocative new shape underscored by Muller's sense of irony and even kitsch. This act of reinvention is necessary to Muller's vision, because in the discarded he sees deeper meaning and continued life. Transformed by the perspective he brings, the objects, through the wondrous and insightful vision of this artist, are reshaped and assembled. Muller's special gift for seeing life in the world around him leads him to create playfully rebellious spirits who shatter mundane colors, shapes, and lines. Simultaneously, these spirits act as a generous host, like a chanteuse quietly awaiting an opportunity to delight, provoke, seduce, or charm the unwitting person who enters.

The seeming calm is actually brimming over and transforming into a kind of interior gurgle, [with] slight cracks in the under- and overtones of [a] deep, resonant voice oozing out of those undone seams, [releasing] a wild and raw energy. The body that was, at first sight, purposefully calm and fully integrated, is now oscillating multi-directionally and poly-temporally [to] its own cacophonous accompaniment, with the strange and natural order of them, the rightness that only they can have.

– KAREN BAMONTE

In a piece where many of the objects are recognizable, but the arrangement is unfamiliar, one gets the impression of a dreamed constellation, hovering illuminated in space, challenging us to consider its newly conceived purpose. Exploration gives way to expression, and we observe the art of a mature mind, one as skilled at listening to objects as providing them with a stage on which to speak for themselves.

The mountains, trees, and water along the journey can then, to the eye accustomed to seeing things uniquely, be transformed along with the rest of the world around them. The same forest can be either a commonplace grove of trees or a wilderness of delight, vivid, and extraordinary, the difference being the perception of the viewer. At the end of this journey, we see the entire collage of objects anew, brought together in a new construction, the inner landscape of their world divulged to us by Muller with a conspiratorial wink. Water is once again water, and we see that something essential has remained constant throughout the journey. But although a teacup may still be a teacup, neither the artist nor the spectator can ever see a teacup in quite the same way again.

these contraptions, floating, squatting, flying, are seers,

fortune tellers, look, travel, look here, adventure, look, love.

because red wings can flap on copper spirals,

lifting up even the heaviest head,

lifting up even the largest shovel known to man,

lifting up even the most waterlogged, landlocked, sluggish prayers

to the most amazing pantheon...

A BRIEF CATALOGUE OF
SELECTED WORKS, 1993–2008

COMMENTARY BY WARREN MULLER

ENDURING VISION

As 1 dream for myself, 1 dream for others. Others who long for happiness, and life to reveal in itself a vitality that cannot contain itself. And 1 search for others who dream for me. 1 trust the laughter and affection, the eyes that glow with a fire that lusts for a future grander than we can imagine. 1 celebrate the journey and the stops along the way. Signposts that say, this is the way—continue believing.

1 dream of making art that is alive. That speaks back to me and others. Not knowing exactly what it is saying—knowing that it is speaking is enough. Trusting that 1 will understand enough to continue and keep making more.

F ATE BROUGHT ME to Philadelphia. 1970. A time to reinvent the world. Everything seemed possible. The city was crumbling, abandoned. I aspired to see what I could invent starting from scratch, picking up the pieces of basic human nature and things left to rust and decompose. All ready to be reborn. Never before had I seen so many of my age so willing to experiment and create the future.

No one wanted those buildings or their contents. Few were doing business on abandoned streets. The storefronts invited us to display whatever we could put together from what we found. And I was so at home in a storefront. I had spent my childhood in my parents' dry cleaning business playing store. Just a continuation. No need to grow up. Dreams emerging from whatever would present itself.

And whatever we created, we called it Art. And Art didn't mind. It seemed as if we couldn't fail. The world was already imploding. What did we have to lose?

On the other side of this great surge of energy was a great sadness that the world before us, the one passed down, was falling apart and did not offer any hope at all. We had to reinvent it or just give up everything. We conspired to create hope for the future, searching for a new language that we could call our own—a language that we could call Art.

The following represents some of my major works, commissions, and exhibitions over the last fifteen years. By no means exhaustive, it is an opportunity to reflect and take stock. It's exciting to look back. Even more exciting to look ahead…

WM: "When I first saw this, I said to Isaiah, 'It doesn't look like me.' He told me, 'Don't worry, you'll grow into it.' He was right.

43

001. *Orange Crush*, 2005
15 × 20 x 20 feet (4.6 × 6 x 6 meters), mixed media, incandescent lighting
Collection of the artist

WM: " 'Orange Crush' was a large installation at Swarthmore College's List Gallery—it spanned floor to ceiling. The room was painted
orange to give the sensation of being inside a bottle of Orange Crush soda. You could almost taste the orange light."

002. *Lighter Ladder*, 2003
8 × 2 feet (244 × 61 cm), mixed media, fiber optic lighting
Collection of the artist

WM: "This piece represents my first experiment with fiber optics. The light source is a metal halide bulb directed
through the fiber optics. A motorized filter causes the color to undulate gently back and forth."

003. *Pogo's Charm Bracelet*, 1998 (right)
10 × 3 feet (305 × 91 cm), mixed media, incandescent lighting
Collection of the artist

WM: "At the bottom left of the piece is a violin from the late Asher Zagar, Isaiah's father. Pogo, the namesake of the sculpture, is the blue lamb at the top. This was the beginning of a series of bracelets attached to chains."

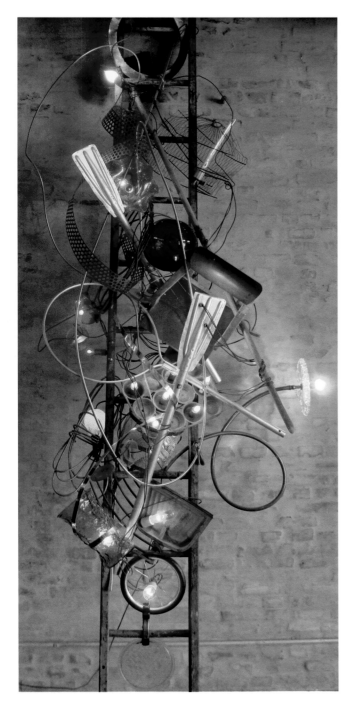

004. *Litter Ladder*, 2004 (left)
4 × 12 × 1 feet (122 × 357 × 30 cm),
mixed media, incandescent lighting
Collection of the artist.

WM: "Part of my Ladders of Light series—an ongoing series waiting for the next 'right' ladder to appear. Created to span floor to ceiling, the litter has the effect of confusing the orientation; you aren't sure whether the light is ascending or descending."

005. *Symphony*, 2003
20 × 5 x 5 feet (6 × 1.5 x 1.5 meters), mixed media, incandescent lighting
Collection of Lis Kalogris

WM: *"This was the first of many commissions for Lis and Michael Kalogris, who I later would come to know as my First Patrons. As a working artist for my entire adult life, I had always wondered what the term "art patron" really meant. They continue to show me the answer to that: possibility."*

LIS KALOGRIS: "There is a flurry of art and craft everywhere in our home but, at its core, there is *Symphony*. It is the magnet that draws guests into the center of our universe. The sculpture moves between the floors of our home, blending our private space with the spaces we share. No one enters our home without commenting on *Symphony*. People gather around it and connect with its magic—it cuts through all social lines. Everyone seems to have a grandmother or aunt who owns the exact same blue glass pitcher hanging from the piece. Then I tell them about the golden globe in the center—that it came from a chandelier that formerly hung in Saks—that they were renovating the store and threw away the old to make way for the new. Typically, all those who set eyes on *Symphony* plan to leave our kitchen and go

home and scavenge their basements for old stuff to light up. How hard could it be? Aha! Be sure to take another look, because it is not all about magic: It is also a delightfully calculated fusion of art and craft. It is a feat of engineering, a skillful execution, beautifully balanced, secure, sensual (or a little sexy)—a veritable symphony. *Symphony* was conceived the first time I set eyes on Warren Muller. It was some eight years ago, and we met in his extraordinary lighting studio on Third Street. Warren exuded confidence and sweetness, and I was mad about him and his light sculptures—I took the plunge. I have been joyously bathed in the light of Warren Muller and his work ever since. I live with seven works created from his unique blending of form and function in art and light."

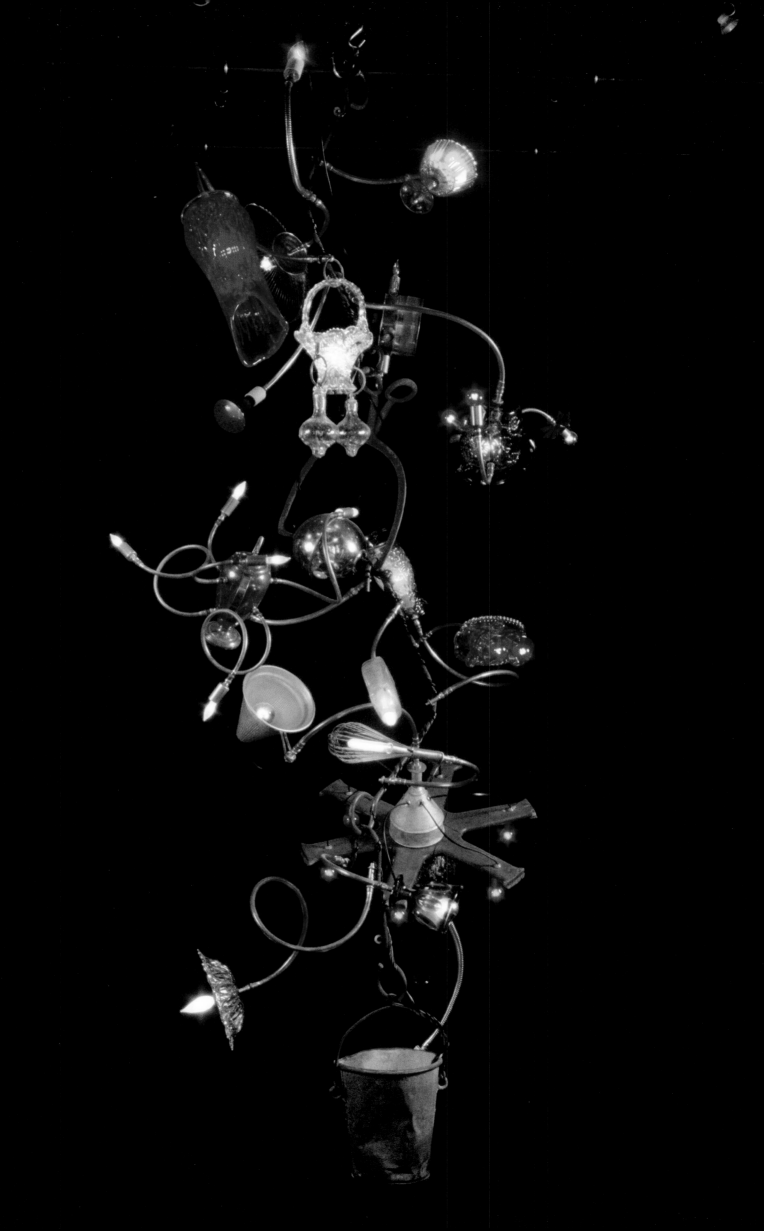

006. *Mr. Lucky's Tiara*, 2004

9 × 3.5 x 1 feet (274 × 107 x 30 cm), mixed media, incandescent lighting

Collection of Lis Kalogris

LIS KALOGRIS: "'Mr. Lucky's Tiara' he called it. Some guy won the lottery and commissioned the piece and then disappeared into thin air—hence the title."

007. *Big Wheel*, 2008
48 × 48 × 36 inches (122 × 122 x 91 cm), mixed media, incandescent lighting
Collection of Melissa and Ben Rayer

*WM: "I figured this might give the Rayer's three children a slightly different perspective
on some of their toys."*

008. *Roll Me a Fatty*, 2008

48 × 36 × 30 inches (122 × 91 x 76 cm), mixed media, incandescent lighting

Private collection

WM: *"This was the first piece I made in the new studio space on North American Street."*

009. *Stonewall*, 2007

8 × 10 x 9 feet (244 x 305 × 274 cm), mixed media, incandescent lighting

Stonewall Country Club, Elverson, PA

WM: "I said to RJ, "Are you sure I'm the right person to do this? A country club?"'

RJ THORNBURG: "There was no doubt in my mind from the moment I set foot in the country club—I knew that Warren's work would completely transform the space that the restaurant currently occupied. A former design client and member of the golf club had called me in because the space lacked any appeal whatsoever. It looked like a religious convention hall, with hunter-green everything, almost no light, and oppressive volumes of empty space framed in oak.

"The building shell itself was a richly historic dairy barn dating from the 1800s, part of a "gentleman's farm" belonging to the Pew family. Like most country clubs, it gave the appearance of being staid and stuffy. "We need to do something that will make our members and their spouses want to dine here," was the message from the manager.

"Warren's work was the key to the success of the renovation. As with anything that has the possibility of being unexpected, the installation of these works created a buzz. The club became a destination for members and their guests, who still claim to see something new every time they experience the space. And lunch and dinner business shot up by 300 percent!"

010. *Milky Way*, 2004

36 × 48 × 12 inches (91 × 122 x 30 cm), mixed media, incandescent lighting

Collection of the artist

WM: "Part of the Container of Light series. 'Milky Way' is an old-fashioned milk crate with single-serving, recyclable milk bottles the milkman used to deliver. As a kid I remember a friend's dad owned a milk company and delivered bottles like these to our door."

011. *Moxie*, 2001 (right)

24 × 18 × 32 inches (61 × 46 x 81 cm), mixed media, incandescent lighting. Collection of Bruce Coons.

WM: *"Moxie is the oldest carbonated soda in the US which is still produced, and is Maine's state beverage. A meat hook fit nicely in the original handle holes of the wooden crates."*

012. *Milk Delivery*, 2002 (left)

4 × 3 x 2 feet (122 × 91 x 61 cm), mixed media, incandescent lighting. Collection of the artist.

WM: *"The hand truck was given by a Philadelphia neighbor, who had just closed a 100-year-old machinery business. The hand truck is imaginarily pushing the crate of milk forward, and is a type of performance sculpture used in the 2003 Philadelphia Fringe Festival."*

013. *EZ Chair*, 2004
60 × 24 x 36 inches (152 × 61 x 91 cm), mixed media, incandescent lighting
Collection of Bahdeebahdu

014. *Marcel du Lamp*, 2000 (top right)
24 × 18 × 32 inches (61 × 46 x 81 cm), mixed media, incandescent lighting. Collection of the artist.

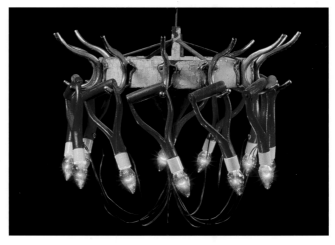

015. *Clam Rake*, 2005 (bottom right)
36 × 18 × 12 inches (91 × 46 x 30 cm), mixed media, incandescent lighting. Collection of Tony Lofrumento and Brad Fowler.

WM: "A gift to dear friends. Their home is in Provincetown. Tongue-in-cheek, but very apropos."

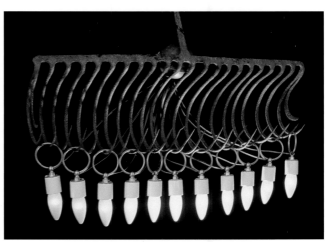

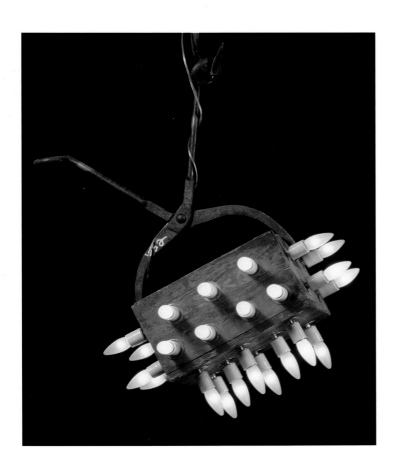

016. *Ice Box*, 1999 (left)
36 × 18 × 14 inches (91 × 46 x 36 cm), mixed media, incandescent lighting. Collection of Warren Holzman.

WM: "This was from the Warren+Warren exhibit at the Bahdeebahdu gallery. He got this piece and I got an stunning steel sculpture of his, a gigantic baby head entitled Hard Labor. An excellent trade."

017. *Auger Light*, 2005 (left)
12 × 8 × 6 inches (30 × 20 x 15 cm), mixed media, incandescent lighting. Private collection..

018. *Rubber Stamp*, 2004 (right)
24 × 18 × 32 inches (61 × 46 x 81 cm), mixed media, incandescent lighting. Private collection.

019. *Elbow Room*, 2004

36 × 48 × 12 inches (00 × 00 cm), mixed media, incandescent lighting

Collection of Ernie Sesskin and Brian Foster

WM: "The elbow came from a laboratory and was intended for industrial use. Filled with glass and plastic objects it takes on a life of its own."

020. *Pink Pussy*, 2004 (above)
30 × 30 × 30 inches (76 × 76 × 76 cm), mixed media, incandescent lighting
Collection of Leslie and David Matthews

WM: *"The Pink Pussy started around a pink squeeze toy. David and Leslie made me promise that what I made for them was quirky, colorful, and fun-filled. That was easy ."*

021. *Pee Wee*, 2004 (right)
60 × 60 × 36 inches (152 × 152 × 91 cm), mixed media, incandescent lighting
Collection of the artist

WM: *"I never seem to tire of making a marriage of the most inane, disparate, and unlikely elements. Kind of like what makes for an interesting party."*

022. *Gravy Boat*, 2002
36 × 48 × 12 inches (91 × 122 x 30 cm), mixed media, incandescent lighting
Private collection

023. *Kitchen Constellation*, 2002

36 × 48 × 48 inches (91 × 122 x 122 cm), mixed media, incandescent lighting

Private collection

024. *FUN-nels*, 1999 (above)
36 × 36 x 36 inches (91 × 91 x 91 cm), mixed media, incandescent lighting
Collection of Donna Leonard

WM: "This was commissioned for the restaurant Il Buco, on Bond Street in New York."

025. *Dairy D-Lite*, 2002 (opposite)
96 × 60 inches (244 × 152 cm), mixed media, incandescent lighting
Collection of Jason Olim

 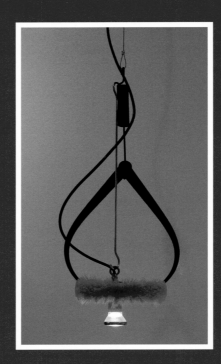 

026. *Shoe Fetish*, 2005 (above left)
18 × 12 inches (46 × 30 cm), mixed media,
incandescent lighting. Collection of
RJ Thornburg and Warren Muller.

027. *Caliper Bush*, 2005 (above center)
18 × 12 inches (46 × 30 cm), mixed media,
incandescent lighting. Collection of
RJ Thornburg and Warren Muller.

028. *Basket Case*, 2005 (above right)
18 × 12 inches (46 × 30 cm), mixed media,
incandescent lighting. Collection of
RJ Thornburg and Warren Muller.

029. *Pendant Lambps*, 2000 (right)
40 × 20 inches (102 × 51 cm), mixed media,
incandescent lighting. Collection of Gina Zegel.

WM: *"The smaller works resemble my sketches. They keep my hands
busy while seeming to make themselves. I am often thinking they
are part of a bigger picture or piece that I might be contemplating.
Then someone comes into my studio and wants it as it is."*

030. *Lamb a la Cart*, 2004
36 × 48 × 12 inches (90 × 120 × 30 cm), mixed media, incandescent lighting
Collection of Martin Kline

031. *Bull Lit*, 2004
48 × 30 inches (122 × 76 cm), mixed media, incandescent lighting
Commissioned by Phillip E. Smith;
collection of Eve-Marie and Peter Schaffer

WM: *"One of my favorite pieces which I would have kept for myself. This was the fruit of collaboration between designer, client, and artist."*

032. *Blue Light Special*, 2001
48 × 36 x 24 inches (122 × 91 x 61 cm), mixed media, incandescent lighting
Private collection

033. *Crystal Blue Persuasion*, 2001

36 × 15 inches (91 × 38cm), mixed media, incandescent lighting

Collection of the artist

WM: *"While kicking around the yard of a bottle factory, I unearthed this chunk of*
blue slag glass. I held it up to the light... a keeper."

034. *Empty Basket*, 2004 (right)
36 × 24 inches (91 × 61 cm), mixed media, incandescent
lighting. Collection of Audrey A.P. Lavin, Ph.D.

035. *Traveling Light*, 2005 (below left, top)
24 × 26 × 12 in (61 × 66 x 30 cm), mixed media,
incandescent lighting. Collection of Peter and Judy Leone

036. *Rib Light*, 2002 (below left, bottom)
00 × 00 inches (00 × 00 cm), mixed media, incandescent
lighting. Private Collection

037. *Shop Rite Light*, 2001 (below right)
00 × 00 inches (00 × 00 cm), mixed media, incandescent
lighting. Collection of Lis and Mike Kalogris

WM: *"These pieces are a continuation of the Duchamp tribute series. I often refer to them as my 'one-liners,' pieces that are already 'a thing' as it exists or in the condition that I find it. Often I can see the piece right away, but at other times I only 'discover' it after it's been hanging up for months...even years."*

038. *Test Case*, 2002

12 × 24 inches (30 × 61 cm), mixed media, incandescent lighting

Collection of RJ Thornburg

WM: "Lighting an odd space is never a problem when you work with a designer who tells you to simply use an odd light."

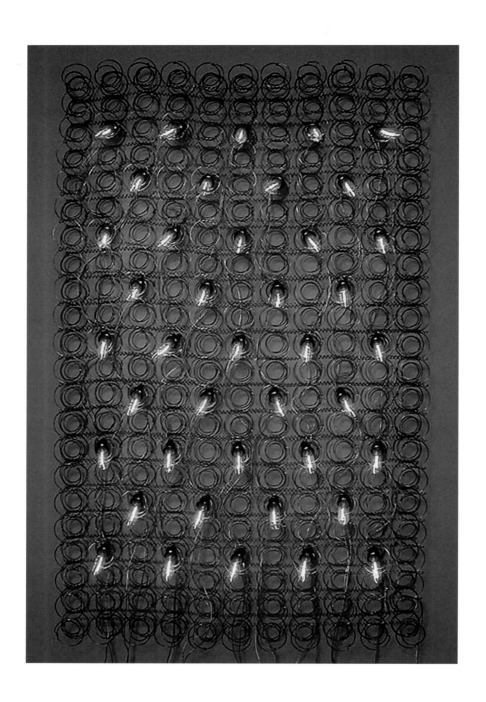

039. *Light Sleep*, 2004
84 × 60 inches (213 × 152 cm), mixed media, incandescent lighting
Collection of Lynn Buono and Skip Schwarzman

040. *Light Form 36-24-36*, 2006
48 × 18 inches (122 × 46 cm), mixed media, incandescent lighting
Collection of the artist

041. *Tingly*, 2004 (above)
48 × 12 inches (122 × 30 cm), mixed media, Lutron lighting
Collection of the artist, special event exhibit

042. *Wired Up*, 2004 (right)
84 × 72 × 60 inches (213 × 182 x 152 cm), mixed media, incandescent lighting
Collection of the artist

WM: *"I wanted to create my own version of netting–a threaded pattern, yet airy, web-like and transparent. After I finished
the framework, Isaiah stopped in and said, 'It needs rain.' Then I knew what the light should look like."*

043. *Animal Dreamland*, 2003

84 × 48 inches (213 × 122 cm), mixed media, incandescent lighting

Collection of the artist

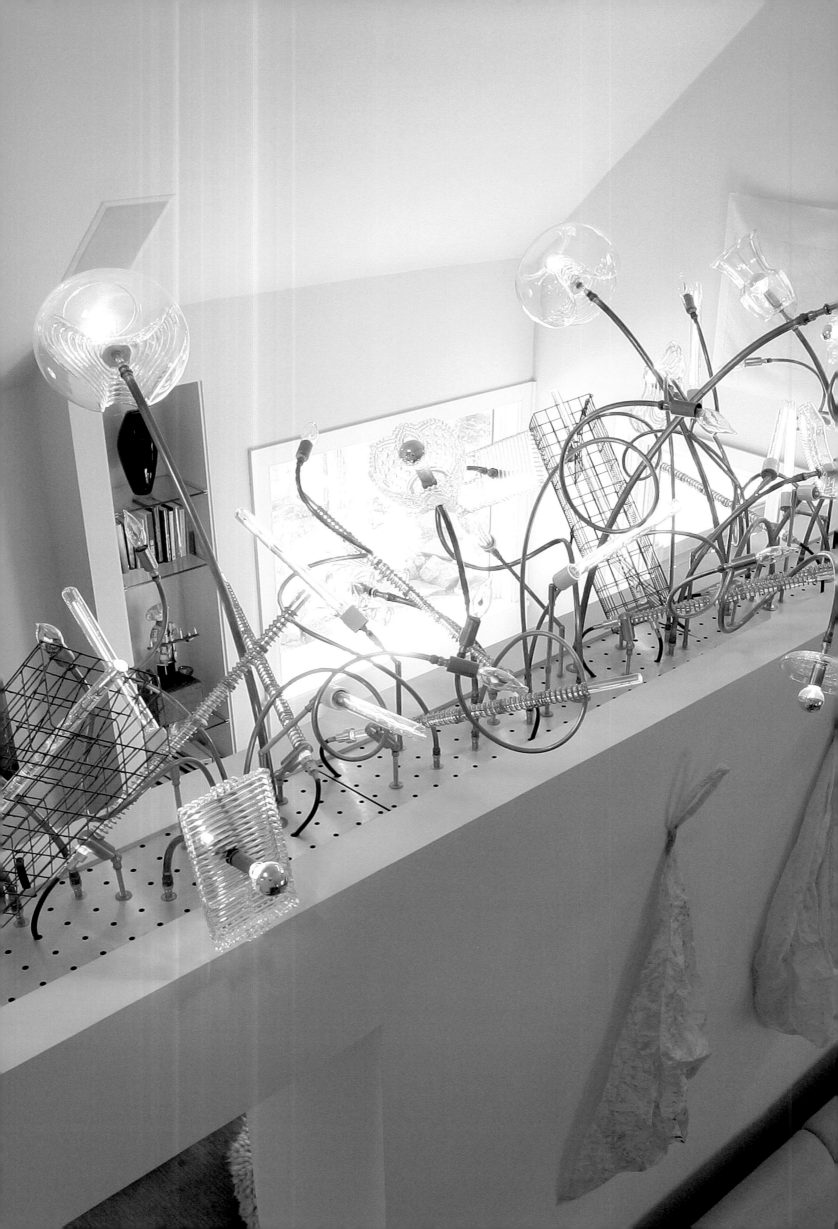

044. *Light Garden*, 2002
180 × 60 inches (457 × 172 cm), mixed media, incandescent and fiber optic lighting
Collection of Lis and Michael Kalogris

WM: "My vision for this room was that the lighting would appear like an interior garden inspired by the natural woodland setting of the house. The objective was to have multiple ambiences for various moods and light qualities throughout the day."

LIS KALOGRIS: "This sculpture is nearly twelve linear feet of copper pipe, plates and cups, globes from my old dining room fixture, fiber-optically lighted cylinders, wire baskets, and fascinating light bulbs—a giant garden planter having been submerged into the wall, with 'plants' emitting their glow throughout the room. Warren's great gift is his sense of fluidity and balance. I believe the core of his more recent work is connected to the way dancers move their bodies. Then he adds a touch of whimsy and perfectly artful 'carelessness.' Through this piece, he also shares with us another of his gifts—his ability to see what can be made magnificent from castoffs and rejectables."

045. *My Hope's Light*, 2003

84 × 60 x 48 inches (213 × 154 x 122 cm), mixed media, incandescent lighting

Collection of Hope and Paul Makler

WM: "Getting this commission was like getting the best prize in a box of Cracker Jacks. I went to the house, and Hope
pointed to the ceiling in the dining room and said, "I want to replace this Calder with one of your pieces."
There was a Schnabel on the wall beyond. The thought that I had arrived crossed my mind."

046. *Twirling Flowers*, 2001
48 × 48 x 12 inches (122 × 122 x 30 cm), mixed media, incandescent lighting
Collection of Lis Kalogris

WM: "This was an opportunity to make that little trip to the powder room a far more interesting excursion!"

047. *It's Raining Zen*, 2004 (above)
36 × 12 inches (91 × 30 cm), mixed media, incandescent lighting
Collection of Lis and Michael Kalogris

WM: *"The glass I found in a glass factory refuse pile. Transport vehicles had driven over the recently fired glass, both flattening and making an impression on it. "*

048. *Tiffany Vision*, 2004 (right)
30 × 72 inches (74 × 182 cm), mixed media, incandescent lighting
Commissioned by Barbara Tiffany; collection of Gwen and David Keiser

WM: *"This commission was challenging in that I was asked to design a piece to share stage with another piece of artwork— I wasn't afforded my regular 'air time.' But the pieces fit well together—just like old friends."*

049. *King and Queen of Dreams I (of a pair)*, 2006
72 × 60 x 48 inches (182 × 154 x 122 cm), mixed media, incandescent lighting
Collection of Meg and Peter Saligman

WM: "Made from the family's collection of crystal chandeliers and reconfigured around a wire cylindrical cage.
Two crystal chandeliers were reused in their entirety in this new configuration."

RJ THORNBURG: "This was an opportunity to work on a house with a remarkable, historically correct restoration. I've never done anything like it. The client, a public works artist with a wild, larger-than-life vision, had a notion that the interiors could be less than accurate. We helped convince Meg and Peter to 'take ownership' of their home and its design. She imagined grandiose chandeliers for the house and even gave the originals to Warren to use. The result was 'hysterically' correct, and so much more interesting."

050. *Il Sogno (The Dream)*, 2005
96 × 48 inches (243 × 122 cm), mixed media, incandescent lighting
Collection of Sam and Dena Lombardo

WM: "This work was commissioned by a couple in Lancaster, PA, not the kind of place where my work is well known. But after speaking with the Lombardos at length, it became clear that this piece was a significant part of what they wanted to express in their home, and they enthusiastically commissioned us."

RJ THORNBURG: "During the process of working with Sam and Dena on the design of their new home were discussions about what to do with the volume of space and the views from within, above, and outside looking in. The architect had made some very safe and conservative recommendations prior to my walking into the project. In my design world (since meeting Warren), nothing puts the uniqueness into a project more than Warren's amazing sculptures—they deal with the space, create conversation, and serve a functional purpose. The clients were willing to 'sign up' and push the limits of the usual local fare. Everything after that just fell into place."

051. *Mallet Orb*, 1998 (above)

30 × 30 × 30 inches (76 × 76 x 76 cm), mixed media, incandescent lighting

Collection of Peter Saligman

WM: "This was the last of a series of gritty, tougher pieces. It looked like a wrecking ball that had picked up everything along its way. You can almost see the light of the grime.

052. *Oh Morrie*, 2002 (right)

120 × 108 × 96 inches (306 × 275 x 244 cm), mixed media, incandescent lighting

Commissioned by Morrie Breyer, designer; collection of Jackie and Skip Morgan

WM: "The entire house was built of disassembled barns. This commission pushed all the limits of scale and complexity I had experienced up until then. I had to find a temporary space to accommodate the dimensions of this piece, and that later became my permanent studio. After working on this, size mattered less and less. The finished piece was shipped to Utah for installation."

053. *Baby Needs a New Pair of Shoes*, 2000

48 × 36 inches (122 × 91 cm), mixed media, incandescent lighting

Collection of Red Tettemer

WM: "This advertising firm with a very starched-collar clientele was willing to push the limits of their image in the corporate world, restructuring to embrace a more dynamic vision. They called on me to help them find a way to loosen up and have fun."

054. Scribble, 2008

240 × 120 inches (610 × 305 cm), mixed media, incandescent lighting

The Philadelphia Building, Philadelphia, PA

*WM: "Tony Goldman does what I do, but with buildings. He takes what's been disregarded, ignored,
and nearly discarded, sees its value, and brings it back to life."*

TONY GOLDMAN: "Experiencing Warren's work for the first time on a studio visit, after being encouraged to go by my colleague, Craig Grossman, I was immediately convinced that Warren had the artistic ability, aesthetic talent, and creativity to be considered for a major commission. We are collectors and have always incorporated art in our properties.

"For this commission, we wanted to reposition The Philadelphia Building as a building that would attract tenants within the 'creative cut' of their profession. In order to make that case, we needed to be bold, unique, and willing to incorporate the unexpected. Warren has that absolute ability within his sculptural imagination to implement and execute the unexpected. I saw in his work that he could take a distinctive position, through the selection of particular, unique materials and related findings, and create a clear and abstract sculptural point of view.

"In this case, we selected glass as the unifying material, and Warren magnificently crafted more than a half dozen works, large and small, that now adorn the building. With his works presently installed throughout the building, Warren's creations have successfully helped us achieve the goals we originally set out to attain by artistically differentiating the look and feel of our environments. Warren is an artist with exceptional talent."

055. *Steer It Up*, 2008

64 × 78 × 65 inches (163 × 198 × 165 cm), mixed media, incandescent lighting

2008 PSPCA DogHaus, Chestnut Hill, PA

WM: "I made this piece for a room that RJ designed for DogHaus, a designer show house
in Chestnut Hill that benefits the Pennsylvania SPCA."

056. *Minimasterpiece*, 2007

180 × 144 x 168 inches (457 × 366 × 427 cm), mixed media, incandescent lighting

Collection of the artist and Gabor Antalics

WM: "It started one day as a joke. I challenged my friend, Gabor, who imports old Rovers, Minis, and Morris Minors, to get me one so I could make a chandelier. We really yukked it up. I continued to chide him about it whenever we got together. About a year later he showed up with a flatbed truck, car in tow. A 60s Mini. The joke got to the punch line. He offered his garage to work on the piece, and my assistant Rebecca and I got right to work. An opportunity to exhibit the sculpture at the Philadelphia Cruise Ship Terminal's Navy Yard was all we needed to motivate us to completion. Several months later, at almost a ton and a half, my biggest piece to date was being unveiled. Now we're thinking about an Airstream."

GABOR ANTALICS: "I had been importing 'classic' Austin Mini automobiles for years, and I used to park my favorite blue Mini 1000 outside Warren's studio, which may have sowed the original seed in his head. I was able to find, through the 'Mini grapevine', a wonderful pea-soup green 1964 Countryman (the 'woody wagon') in an old barn near West Chester, Pennsylvania. The only passengers were a few surprised mice, and after dragging it out with a tractor, I realized just how perfect it was, rodent nest and all. We got it back to the shop, and I removed the engine and gearbox, and impaled it with a large steel I-beam; a crazy olive on a toothpick. We hoisted it up, yelled 'watch your feet,' and there it was—four little tires swinging in the air. Warren worked his magic, and as a finishing touch—and contrary to everything I know about British car electrics—I was able to get the headlamps and tail lights burning bright after 45 years. Thankfully, Warren stopped me before I tried to get the horn and radio working..."

the buddhas with rabbit heads, the quan yins gone david,

the tarot card masters with cloves and tails

imagine where these gods could take your prayers.

illumined polished gilded, suspended

turned green, transformed into plant matter

hovering in the homiest places

galaxies in kitchens and domestic solar systems...

"I first met Patsy Ratchet (Warren's alter-ego) when my band was playing music for Warren and and Isaiah Zagar's 50th birthday celebration. What a night! Strange Woofy Bubbles puppets floating about the room, men in drag, women in drag, Isaiah's aged parents sitting demurely enjoying some cake. In the band that night was a young drummer fresh out of Kansas City via the Curtis Institute. During breaks, the young man was quite distraught by all the goings-on and I felt like I was talking him down from an acid trip, 'It's OK. It's OK. The puppets are good.'"

— HEATH ALLEN, MUSICIAN

«Almost a self portra Warren's creations characters that wou show up in your livi room. It's not a te cup, but a cup of lig What brings light a performance togeth is digging into the ser of complete abando ment and immersi in the work, and lovi the fallibility of it.»

— MELANIE STEWA
PERFORMANCE ART

«When looking at Warren's work, I am struck with a sense of wonder and awe. To be able to take materials otherwise destined for the trash and create a thing of such beauty is truly a gift.»

— MICHAEL ARIZIN, COLLECTOR

"Most nights we sit below Warren's piece and eat dinner with our two children. We are endlessly entertained by it, often ending dinner with 'the Light Game,' played by naming the objects in the piece. It never gets old."

— LESLIE MATTHEWS, COLLECTOR

"He takes all of these unrelated, disparate things—discarded, orphaned, lonely, ignored, dull, heinous even—and begins the process of connecting them. He is this big kid in the biggest toy box, with endless imagination and ideas."

— RJ THORNBURG

"What elevates his work from me craftsmanship is his visionary outloc his ability to rearrange objects and i corporate an iconography of myth fairytales, and personal idiosyncrasie Motion change and improvisation a implied in these works—stars and te cups fly through the universe, ps chedelic swirls of energy expand an contract—like a glimpse of chaos cap tured and frozen for a split second

— DEBORAH SCOBLIONKOV, WRI

o call them chandeliers would be too easy. ...ey were totally improbable, totally origi- ...l inventions. Sometimes the result of a ...alogue with a client who supplied some ... the materials. More often the result of ... conversation Warren was having with ...mself. Warren got light to be more than ...st illumination. He got it to tell a story."

— RICK SNYDERMAN, SNYDERMAN-WORKS GALLERIES

«There is then, a rather perverse and inverse relationship between Warren Muller, the person, and his art. It's as if both the personal and artistic emotional tracks are part of an enormously long crossfade that will last a lifetime. These two tracks are waxing and waning, dancing and singing their way in between the worlds of distillation, integration, and harmony, and the more carnal realm of maximality, chaos and wildness. Warren Muller and his art seem to be walking the line between the light and the dark, with at least one toe tapping in time, right over the edge...taking a walk on the wild side.»

— KAREN BAMONTE, PERFORMANCE AND VISUAL ARTIST

...hen Warren danced, he ...s freedom personified— ... arms and legs and torso ...raling through space... ...me to think of it, he ...oved a lot like his not-yet- ...nceived-of chandeliers..."

— MICHAEL BIELLO,
INTERDISCIPLINARY ARTIST

«I can't speak for Warren's work any better than it speaks for itself — in soft riddles and twinkling jests, playful reminiscences and various sharp objects...»

— PAUL SCHNEIDER, WRITER

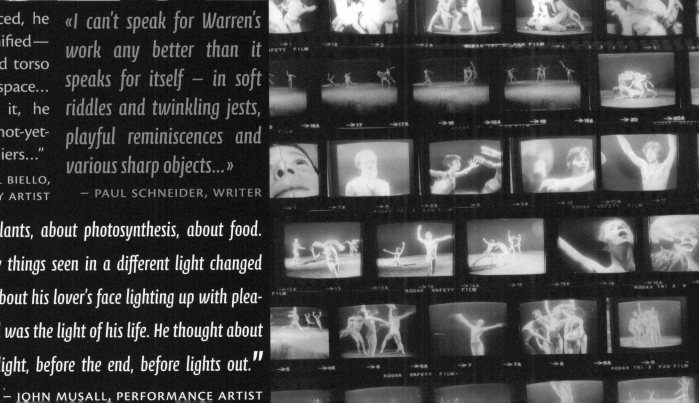

...e thought about plants, about photosynthesis, about food. ... thought about how things seen in a different light changed ...aning. He thought about his lover's face lighting up with plea- ...e, and how that soul was the light of his life. He thought about ...nging the truth to light, before the end, before lights out."

— JOHN MUSALL, PERFORMANCE ARTIST

CHRONOLOGY

1946

Born in Royal Hospital, Bronx, New York, to Irving and Lillian Muller. Grows up in a predominantly Eastern European neighborhood in the Bronx with his grandmother, aunts, cousins, and sister. Grandfather owns an ornamental ironwork factory, where Warren has an opportunity to observe him at work. Parents buy a dry cleaning business in the Bronx.

1956

Family moves to the suburbs in Yonkers, New York. First workshop created out of garage. Warren begins his collection of things that he deconstructs to see how they are put together. Assembles first debris sculptures in gutters which young Muller didn't consider 'completed' until the rains came and the flash floods transformed them into their final form. First experiments with performance art using the unclaimed clothes from the racks at the dry cleaning store.

1965

Attends Hartford Art School and studies painting and sculpture. Travels to Greece and attends Aegean School of Fine Arts

while living on the isle of Paros. Returns to the United States and attends Philadelphia College of Art. Receives BFA in film and photography. Works with Berlin dancers Manfred Fischbeck and Brigitta Herrmann, first as a documentary filmmaker, then as a backdrop artist and dancer.

1972

Muller meets artists and community builders Julia and Isaiah Zagar, who inspire a life-long collaborative relationship. He joins Woo World Players as a performance artist. Both of Muller's parents die within one year of each other. Performs at the Philadelphia Museum of Art with Woo World Players in "Futurism and the International Avant Guard." Makes first road trip out West, spending a month in Aspen, Colorado, where he performed. Buys a house in Telluride, returning the following year for a two-year stint. Performs in Men's Dance Festival with Lucas Hoving Dance Company in San Francisco. Meets Philip Yenawine during his time in Colorado.

1981

Performs in Gerhardt Knoedel's exhibition "Inside Out." Creates "Sacred Walnut" in collaboration with Karen Bamonte. Presents sculptural and performance works at Painted Bride Art Center in Philadelphia. Exhibits at Convergence Gallery, New York City.

1986

Travels to Berlin, Germany. Sets up a studio at the Berlin Wall. Paints series "Sink or Swim." Exhibits at Moritzplatz Gallery. Performs in East Berlin Oranionbar with Jac Carley and Ric Schachtebeck. Returns to New York to perform as guest artist in "Sex and Dance" with Melanie Stewart Dance at P.S. 122 in New York City.

1987

Moves to New York City, renting Lower East Side storefront studio. Creates Theatre of Relativity with writer-director John Musall.

2002

Meets partner RJ Thornburg and within a year, they open a new gallery space together on Cherry Street, Bahdeebahdu Studio and Gallery.

2008

Bahdeebahdu Studio moves to a larger warehouse location on North American Street in Philadelphia, which will provide much needed additional exhibition and workshop space and accommodate larger pieces. One month prior to the anticipated move, an electrical fire in the Cherry Street gallery causes extensive damage to fixtures and materials, delaying the move by several months. The new space opens with a gala opening in June.

1990

Opens Bond Street Studio with Michael Biello and Patricia Kelly in New York City. Performs at Museum of Modern Art with Sons and Daughters. Guest Artist with Merce Cunningham Studio in New York, David Rousseve Dance at Brooklyn Academy of Music, and Jim Self at the Serious Fun Festival at Lincoln Center.

1996

Moves back to Philadelphia. Opens Biello-Muller Studio and Gallery on Third Street with Michael Biello. Muller exhibits first light sculptures.

EXHIBITIONS

2007	Philadelphia International Airport, PA
2006	List Gallery, Swarthmore College, PA
2005	Reading Art Works (RAW), Reading, PA
2003	Hunterdon Museum, Hunterdon, NJ
2001	Robeson Gallery, Penn State University, PA
1999	Gallery Joe, Philadelphia, PA
	John Elder Gallery, New York, NY
1998	Painted Bride Art Center, Philadelphia, PA
	Cortland Jessup Gallery, New York, NY
1989–96	Archetype Gallery, New York, NY
1989	Sally Hawkins Gallery, New York, NY
1987-88	M.P. Gallery of Modern Art, New York, NY
1986	Moritzplatz Gallery, Berlin, Germany

1985	San Francisco Arts Festival, San Francisco, CA
	Vorpal Gallery, San Francisco, CA
1984	Fun Gallery, New York, NY
	San Francisco Arts Commission Gallery, CA
1983	Crocker Museum of Art, Sacramento, CA
1982	Convergence Gallery, New York, NY
1981	Smithsonian Institute of Art, Washington, D.C.
	Taft Museum, Cleveland, OH
1980	Dimock Gallery, George Washington University, Washington, D.C.
	Meyer, Breyer, Weiss Gallery, San Francisco, CA
	Tyler School of Art, Temple University, Philadelphia, PA
1979–82	Snyderman Gallery, Philadelphia, PA

WORKS IN PUBLIC SPACES

PUBLIC BUILDINGS

The Philadelphia Building, Philadelphia, PA

Bat Bar, Hong Kong

Painted Bride Art Center, Philadelphia, PA

Guggenheim Museum Tea Salon, New York, NY

RESTAURANTS

Stonewall Country Club, Elverson, PA

Seafood Unlimited, Philadelphia, PA

Supper, Philadelphia, PA

Vong, New York, NY

Il Buco, New York, NY

Bridget Foy's, Philadelphia, PA

Il Ghiottone, Philadelphia, PA

Tres Amici, Ybor City, FL

Flowers, New York, NY

Bow Thai, New York, NY

Tamany Hall, New York, NY

Kwaanza, New York, NY

Arroyo Grille, Philadelphia, PA

Rococo, Philadelphia, PA

Tutto Misto, Philadelphia, PA

BOOKS

Baro, Gene, *Claes Oldenburg: Drawings and Prints* (London: Chelsea House, 1969)

Bell, Tiffany, *Dan Flavin: The Complete Lights, 1961-1996.* (New Haven: Yale University Press, 2004)

Celant, Germano, *Dennis Oppenheim* (Milan: Edizioni Charta, 1997)

Christov-Bakargiev, Carolyn, *Arte Povera.* (New York: Phaidon Press, 1998)

D'Harnoncourt, Anne and Kynaston McShine, editors, *Marcel Duchamp* (New York: Museum of Modern Art, 1973)

Friedlander, Paul, *Rock and Roll: A Social History.* (New York: Westview Press, 1996)

Godfrey, Tony, *Conceptual Art.* (New York: Phaidon Press, 1998)

Osterwold, Tilman, *Pop Art.* (Köln: Taschen Verlag, 1999)

Prather, Marla, *Alexander Calder, 1898-1976* (New Haven: Yale University Press, 1998)

Rotondi, Michael, *James Turrell: The Other Horizon.* (Hatje Cantz Publishers, 2001)

Tomkins, Calvin, *The Bride and the Bachelors: The Heretical Courtship in Modern Art.* (New York: Viking Press, 1976)

_____, *Off the Wall: A Portrait of Robert Rauschenberg.* (New York: Picador Press, 2005)

Violand-Hobi, Heide E., *Jean Tinguely, Life and Work* (Munich: Prestel Verlag, 1995)

Warhol, Andy, *The Philosophy of Andy Warhol: From A to B and Back Again.* (New York: Harvest Books, 1977)

PERIODICALS

Amorosi, A.D., "Green Times Pose a Lighting Challenge," *Philadelphia Inquirer,* 25 April 2008

Donahue, Amy, "Old City Lights Up," *Philadelphia Magazine,* November 1996

Filfield, Kathleen, "The Good Life," *Philadelphia Magazine,* February 2006

Goldsmith, Diane, "A Place to Browse or Boogie," *Philadelphia Inquirer,* 3 January 2003

Jay, Hilary, "One Room Wonder," *Philadelphia Inquirer,* April 2002

Jiang, Julia, "Salvage Art," *Professional Lighting Design* (Beijing Edition), 2008

Rios, Al, "bahdeebahdu," *EnvyMan,* 2006

Schneider, Paul, "An Artist and a Designer Find Their Niche," *New York Times,* 23 June 2006

Philadelphia Home & Garden, 2002

Sokol, David, "Finding Philly," *Elements of Living,* September 2005

Suqi, Rima A., "Trend Watch," *Metropolitan Home,* January 1995

Hogsdon, Moira, "Dining Out Around Manhattan," *New York Observer,* November 1994

"(Some of!) Il Buco's Chandeliers Can Be Yours For a Price," *New York Magazine,* 2007

Grater, Laurel, "Feats of Clay," *Diversions,* 1993

ABOUT THE CONTRIBUTORS

Working out of his Provincetown, Massachusetts, studio, Song of My-self Photography, BRAD FOWLER creates compelling images of people that read true, speak of emotion, and take delight in capturing play-ful, spontaneous moments.

Writer and filmmaker E.C. GRAHAM has lived and worked in Barcelona, Philadelphia, Amman, Damascus, Mexico City, and Kyoto. His indepen-dent film, *La Rosa Negra,* won the second-place prize in the New York Latin American Film Festival, and was the first-prize winner in the Nits de Curtmetratges film festival in Barcelona, where it was chosen to rep-resent Barcelona in the Biennale in Athens, Greece, in 2000. He studied writing at the SOGEM in Mexico City, completed a masters degree at St. John's College in Santa Fe, New Mexico, and is currently completing a sociolinguistic guide to learning and understanding the issues around minority languages, with a focus on the Catalan language.

For an unprecedented second consecutive year, photographer ROBERT HAKALSKI has won one of the top two awards in the Adobe Interna-tional Digital Imaging Competition. Robert's work continues to ex-tend the envelope of computer-based photography and digital design.

KEVIN HANEK is an award-winning New York art director, book de-signer, and packager who has collaborated on book projects with pub-lishers including Rizzoli, Simon & Schuster, Lebhar-Friedman Books, The Free Press, Rutgers University Press, HarperCollins, John Wiley & Sons, Schirmer Books, Kodansha, Sterling, and Smithmark, and in conjunction with such prestigious organizations as the *New York Times,* the American Academy of Chefs, London's Tate Gallery, PBS, The His-tory Channel, and the Culinary Institute of America. His work has been recognized with awards and honors from the New York Book Show, the American Association of University Presses, the International Associa-tion of Culinary Professionals, USA Book News, ForeWord Magazine, and the Independent Publishers Book Awards, among others.

HILARY JAY is an award-winning design journalist, curator, and entre-preneur. In Fall 2000, she was named executive director of The Design Center (TDC) at Philadelphia University, charged with repositioning the institution to reflect the university's broadening design and tech-nology curriculum. Jay has curated and/or produced over 20 exhibi-tions, including the groundbreaking *What Is Design Today?*; *The Graphic Imperative: International Posters for Peace, Social Justice and the Environment*; and Todd Oldham's *Oddities from the Paley Textile Collection.* In 2004, she co-founded DesignPhiladelphia, a week-long, citywide cultural arts festival that advances the public's awareness of design and innovation. Jay serves on the Editorial Board of *Context,* the American Institute of Architecture's quarterly magazine, and her jewelry and home furnish-ings are in the permanent collections of London's Victoria and Albert Museum and the Musée des Arts Decoratifs in Paris.

PAUL SCHNEIDER is the author of *The Adirondacks, A History of America's First Wilderness,* which was a *New York Times* notable book of 1997 and *The Enduring Shore, A History of Cape Cod, Martha's Vineyard, and Nan-tucket,* both published by Henry Holt. Nearly five years in the making, his third book, *Brutal Journey: Cabeza de Vaca and the Epic First Crossing of North America* appeared in May of 2006. He is currently working on a new book about the Depression-era gangsters, Clyde Barrow and Bon-nie Parker, and occasionally contributes to journals and newspapers, most frequently the *New York Times.*

PHILLIP YENAWINE served as director of education at The Museum of Modern Art, New York, for almost a decade, and was on the educa-tion staff of the New York State Council on the Arts, the Metropolitan Museum of Art, and the Museum of Contemporary Art in Chicago. He is the founding director of Visual Understanding in Education (VUE) a nonprofit entity that conducts research in developmentally based education specifically to foster cognitive growth through interaction with art. He was director of museum programs at the South Street Seaport in New York, and founding director of the Aspen Art Museum in Colorado. Yenawine has taught at the Massachusetts College of Art and the University of Illinois, Champaign-Urbana and was a visiting curator for the Institute for Contemporary Art in Boston. Along with many articles and essays, Yenawine is the author of six books about modern art for children and two books for adults also addressing the questions and interests of beginning viewers, *How to Look at Modern Art* and *Key Art Terms for Beginners*. He has been involved with many efforts that support the rights and needs of artists, including Art Matters (a foundation providing fellowships to visual artists) and Visual AIDS (the organization that sponsors Day Without Art and the Red Ribbon project).

RJ THORNBURG has designed interiors for the hospitality, corporate and residential markets over the past twenty-five years. Utilizing his design finesse, RJ creates distinctive spaces with a refreshingly innovative ap-

proach to style, color and scale. Within his trademark interiors, a harmonious coexistence of art and design reflects RJ's strong beliefs of these essential components. His unlikely combinations result in truly effervescent environments, letting people take the design process a little less seriously (and have a little bit of fun along the way too).

FERAL WILLCOX is a multi-disciplinary artist working in media that begin with the letter P—Poetry, Piano, Pottery, and Pen-and-ink. She is most interested in how Pattern evolves in all of these media. She lives in Gainesville, Florida, where nature is an expert at pattern, and where Kucinich got 22 percent of the 2004 vote.

ACKNOWLEDGMENTS

WM: To RJ, for his love, devotion, and perseverance. Thanks for dreaming with me.

And thanks to all of the following: Eric Graham and Kevin Hanek, for their dedication and enthusiasm in creating this book; Michael Biello and Dan Martin, for their friendship and endurance; Julia and Isaiah Zagar, for family and love of Art; John Musall, our tears shall be as diamonds; Woofy Bubbles, for living life as Art; Manfred Fischbeck and Brigitta Herrmann, for breathing dance into all of us; Karen Bamonte, for a friendship of listening and speaking with clarity; Philip Yenawine, joy and tears forever; Rebecca Pulver, for fearlessness and always being there; Kevin Derrick, for believing in us all; Yoly Teran, for keeping me on track with high spirits; Gabor Antalics, for going where no one else will; Lis and Mike Kalogris, for their generosity and appreciation; Leslie and David Matthews, for their playful kindness; Heath Allen, for the music; Feral Willcox, for life as poetry; Hilary Jay, for patience and thoughtfulness; Avery and Evan Thornburg, for love and laughter; Brad Fowler, for showing us ourselves; Tony Lofrumento, for enduring friendship; Eileen Tognini, for being eternally optimistic; Robert Hakalski, for seeing like no other; Rick and Ruth Snyderman, for their vision of community; the Biello family, for embracing me; Murray Weiss, for education and Philadelphia; Deborah King, for Artistry of words; Floss Barber, Yentl extraodinaire; Lanie Wasserman, my favorite for staying with me; Morrie Breyer, for his vision and trust; Adam Kamens, just always there; Marla Waters, for kisses and laughter… and all the artists, friends, and teachers who have given me my dreams.

INDEX

A

Allen, Heath, 116
Animal Dreamland (2003), 4, 5, 84, 85
Antalics, Gabor, 108
art training, 118
Auger Light (2005), 64

B

Baby Needs a New Pair of Shoes (2000), 102, 103
Bahdeebahdu Studio and Gallery, 15, 119
Bamonte, Karen, 38, 117, 118
Basket Case (2005), 72
Biello, Michael, 32, 37, 117, 119
Biello-Muller Studio, 32, 119
Big Wheel (2008), 52
Blue Light Special (2001), 76
Braque, Georges, 1, 2
Bull Lit (2004), 74–75
Bull's Head (Picasso), 2, 3

C

Caliper Bush (2005), 72
catalogue of works, 43–113
chaos in art, 33–34, 116, 117
Chinese teapot experiments, 28–29
chronology, 118–19
Clam Rake (2005), 63
commentary, by Warren, 43. *See also specific names of works*
composition, of works, 15, 31–32, 37–38
convention, avoidance of, 1, 4

C

creative inventiveness, 1–2
Crystal Blue Persuasion (2001), 77

D

Dairy D-Lite (2002), 70–71
dry cleaning business, 27–28, 43, 118
Duchamp, Marcel, 1, 3–4, 37
Duchamp tribute series, 3, 78

E

early years
    birth, 118
    childhood in Bronx, 27–28, 118
    Chinese teapot experiments, 28–29
    chronology, 118–19
    dry cleaning business, 27–28, 43, 118
    lighting and prop-making work, 28–29
    photographs, 28, 29, 118
Elbow Room (2004), 65
Empty Basket (2004), 78
exhibitions, 120
EZ Chair (2004), 62

F

Fischbeck, Manfred, 30, 37, 118
FUN-nels (1999), 70

G

Goldman, Tony, 105
Graham, E.C., 27–38, 122
Gravy Boat (2002), 68
Group Motion, 30–31

H

Hanek, Kevin, 122
Hell, a Small Start (Tinguely), 3

Herrmann, Brigitta, 30, 118
home, description of, 16–23

I

Ice Box (1999), 63
Il Sogno (The Dream) (2005), 98, 99
inspiration
    childhood influences, 27–29
    Chinatown epiphany, 28–29
    for creating light sculptures, 30–38
    dance training activities for, 30–31
    from Isaiah Zagar, 32–34, 37, 118
    light as, 32
    originality and, 32
    Philadelphia industrial remnants as, 29–30
    Pop Art as, 2–4
    teachers, 37
    20th century creative inventiveness and, 1–2
    for using found objects, 2–4
It's Raining Zen (2004), 92

J

Jay, Hilary, xvii, 122

K

Kalogris, Lis and Michael, 48, 51, 78, 89, 91, 92

King and Queen of Dreams (2006), 94–97

Kitchen Constellation (2002), 69

L

Lamb a la Cart (2004), 73

Light Form (2006), 81

Light Garden (2002), 86–89

light sculptures

    chandeliers and, 34–37, 117

    dance training activities and, 30–31

    evolution of, 30–38

    light characteristics and, 31

    See also specific names of works

Light Sleep (2004), 80

Lighter Ladder (2003), 46

Litter Ladder (2004), 47

M

Mallet Orb (1998), 100

Marcel du Lamp (2000), 3, 63

Matthews, Leslie and David, 66, 116

Milk Delivery (2002), 61

Milky Way (2004), 60

Minimasterpiece (2007), *xi*, *xvii*, 106–13

Moxie (2001), 61

Mr. Lucky's Tiara (2004), 50, 51

Musall, John, 31, 117, 119

My Hope's Light (2003), 90

O

Oh Morrie (2002), 100–101

Oldenburg, Claes, 2, 3, 4

Orange Crush (2005), 44–45

P

parents, 32, 118

Pee Wee (2004), 66–67

Pendant Lambps (2000), 72

Picasso, Pablo, 1, 2–4

Pink Pussy (2004), 66

Pogo's Charm Bracelet (1998), 47

Pop Art, 2–4

public spaces, works in, 120

R

Rib Light (2002), 78

Rocking Pot (Voulkos), 2, 3

Roll Me a Fatty (2008), 53

Rosenquist, James, 2, 4

Rubber Stamp (2004), 64

S

Schneider, Paul, 15–23, 37, 117, 122

Scoblionkov, Deborah, 37, 116

Screwarch Bridge (State II) (Oldenberg),
    2, 3

Scribble (2008), *iv–ix*, 104, 105

Self-portrait in photo booth (1962), 31

Shoe Fetish (2005), 72

Shop Rite Light (2001), 78

Snyderman, Rick, 117

Spring Cheer (Rosenquist), 4

Steer It Up (2008), 106–107

Stewart, Melanie, 116, 119

Stonewall (2007), 54–59

Symphony (2003), 48–49

T

teachers, 37

Test Case (2002), 79

Thornburg, RJ

    about, 122

    collaboration with Muller/Zagar, 4

    collection pieces, 79

    gallery, 15

    on *Il Sogno (The Dream)*, 99

    on *King and Queen of Dreams*, 96

    on *Stonewall*, 58

    Warren and, 15–23, 37, 119

    on Warren's works, 58, 99, 116

Tiffany Vision (2004), 92–93

timeline, 118–19

Tingly (2004), 82

Tinguely, Jean, 3, 4

Traveling Light (2005), 78

Twirling Flowers (2001), 91

W

Wired Up (2004), 82–83

Y

Yenawine, Philip, 1–4, 118, 122

Z

Zagar, Asher, 47

Zagar, Isaiah, 32–34, 37, 116, 118

and the youngest god said,

I was a spirited child

and this electricity could be used for art,

for illumination, for connection.

this electricity could be used for art,

and art could be anywhere,

art could be everywhere....

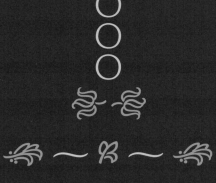

As with the art of Warren Muller, this book has followed an eclectic typographic scheme,
involving several typefaces, each representing a different time period and design aesthetic. Much like that
list of things with which to equip a bride before she makes her trip down the aisle, it uses "something old…"

the captions, copyright page, and commentary text (including this colophon)
have been set in the new Lanston Type Corporation's OpenType version of

LTC *Californian*

a face designed by the prolific American type designer, Frederick Gowdy, as a private commission
for the University of California at Berkeley in 1939, and thought to be one of his finest designs;

"something new…," the title page, section titles, and running heads, as well as commentary
by Warren Muller appearing throughout the book, have been set in the OpenType Pro version of

Adobe Calcite

a sans serif display face by Japanese designer Akira Kobayashi, who first began experimenting with replacing
the openings in the letters of traditional chancery scripts with rigid geometric patterns, resulting in an intriguing
interplay of rounded exterior and angular interior shapes, and a unique synergy of humanism and geometry;

and finally, "something borrowed…"—well, perhaps not in the strictest sense,
but American type designer Robert Slimbach's sans serif type family

Adobe Cronos

used for the running text in this book, does look back to the humanistic, calligraphy-inspired lines
of the work of Renaissance type masters like Claude Garamond and Aldus Manutius, which
continues to have a lasting influence on type design to the present day.

DESIGNED AND COMPOSED BY KEVIN HANEK

PRINTED AND BOUND BY GHP,
WEST HAVEN, CONNECTICUT